Cryptocurrency Trading Guide:

To Altcoins & Bitcoin for Beginners

Top 9 Strategies *to Become Expert in Decentralized Investing Blueprint, Cryptography, Blockchain, DeFi, Mining & Ethereum.*

Crypto Mindset!

provide accurate, up to date and reliable complete

information. No warranties of any kind are expressed or implied. Readers acknowledge that the author is not engaging in the rendering of legal, financial, medical or professional advice. The content of this book has been derived from various sources. Please consult a licensed professional before attempting any techniques outlined in this book.

By reading this document, the reader agrees that under no circumstances are is the author responsible for any losses, direct or indirect, which are incurred as a result of the use of information contained within this document, including, but not limited to, —errors, omissions, or inaccuracies.

" Bitcoin is a very exciting development; it might lead to a world currency. I think over the next decade it will grow to become one of the most important ways to pay for things and transfer assets."

- Kim Dotcom

Book Description

Undeniably, the world economy is becoming a thriving digital ecosystem. Every day there is something new on the internet, whether it is a trend, information, or innovation that can transform some sectors of society. One of these fascinating virtual concepts is cryptocurrency. It is slowly, but steadily changing the global landscape of payment options, trading, and investing.

Lauded as the digital gold of the future, Bitcoin and Altcoins are getting more attention from traditional traders and investors. If you are one of the brave-hearted individuals who are interested to delve into the exciting world of crypto but don't know yet how to start? This book is your compass, your ticket, and your guide to successful entry into the world of virtual currency.

One day, you will tell your own success story. Now is the time to learn, practice, and master the science and art behind the strategies that can help you make a breakthrough. Grab your copy of **Cryptocurrency Trading Guide to Altcoins & Bitcoin for Beginners**: *Learn about Decentralized Investing Blueprint, Cryptography,*

Blockchain, Mining, Ethereum, Litecoin to Create Wealth. Best Trading Strategies.

You are about to enter the future of the digital economy where blockchain and cryptocurrencies are major players. Are you ready?

Table of Contents

Introduction

Cryptocurrency has gone mainstream and changed the economic system by becoming a global phenomenon. Bitcoin and altcoin have captured the attention of businesses, institutional investors, celebrities, and the public in general.

But amidst the buzzing press releases, promotional campaigns, and testimonials of people about cryptocurrencies, it is crucial to understand how crypto works for you.

Learning the basic concepts is your first step to comprehending the exciting world of cryptocurrency. It is the future of the economy, so you might as well embrace it now and master the art of crypto trading and investing.

To help you understand the crypto basics 101 and beyond, I am sharing this book **Cryptocurrency Trading Guide to Altcoins & Bitcoin for Beginners**: *Learn about Decentralized Investing Blueprint, Cryptography, Blockchain, Mining, Ethereum, Litecoin to Create Wealth. Best Trading Strategies.*

It is your roadmap to ensure success whether you trade or invest in cryptocurrency. Every chapter provides vital information that will help you understand this decentralized virtual cash system. Whether we like it or not, the future involves cryptocurrency.

And while it seems complex and technical, the key to understanding the jargon of terms and concepts related to crypto is by learning them by heart. Let your knowledge empower your decisions in diversifying your investment portfolio and harnessing the power of digital gold or cryptocurrency.

But remember that in nature, the cryptocurrency market is wild, fast, and in constant motion. Once you're into crypto trading or investing, it is up to you to master the winning strategies to keep you going and enjoy the 'windfalls' that might come your way.

Are you ready to become the new millionaire or billionaire? Let my book **Cryptocurrency Trading Guide to Altcoins & Bitcoin for Beginners**: *Learn about Decentralized Investing Blueprint, Cryptography, Blockchain, Mining, Ethereum, Litecoin to Create Wealth. Best Trading Strategies* guide to your success. Read on.

Chapter 1

What's All This Buzz About Cryptocurrency?

Bitcoin started it all. This revolutionary, trendsetting cryptocurrency that was introduced in the digital world over a decade ago continues to dominate the scene. When the interest of investors and traders grew, Altcoins or alternative currencies were launched to satisfy the growing needs in the market.

This group of cryptocurrencies is patterned after Bitcoin with a slight alteration of the basic functions and operational rules. The purpose of alternation is to create new cryptocurrencies that serve general or specific functions.

But before we delve in further, let's take a look at the rationale of cryptocurrency and why it is very popular today. This digital currency exists only electronically, so you do not possess physical coins unless you cash them out for tokens. Cryptocurrencies use electronic wallets for storage, eliminating intermediaries like banks.

All transactions are made online, using your computer, mobile phone, or any electronic gadget that allows the exchange of crypto from your end to another user.

At a glance

- ✓ Why are cryptocurrencies very popular?
- ✓ What is cryptocurrency?
- ✓ How does cryptocurrency work?
- ✓ Blockchain technology
- ✓ Peer-to-Peer (P2P) System
- ✓ How did crypto come into being?
- ✓ The creation of new cryptocurrencies
- ✓ Mining: The method of creating new coins of existing cryptocurrencies
- ✓ Are crypto coins and tokens the same?
- ✓ Is cryptocurrency secure and safe to use?
- ✓ Where to store your crypto coins?
- ✓ Ways to acquire crypto coins
- ✓ Frequently Asked Questions (FAQs)

Why are cryptocurrencies very popular?

- They are the currencies of the future.

- They are independent and free from manipulation and interference of any central authority or government.

- They are not governed by central banks, so you don't pay bank charges for your transactions.

- They are not affected by inflation.

- They are useful for quick payments and sensitive transactions.

- They are secured by cryptography which prevents double-spend or counterfeit activities.

- They are digital gold and grow in value over time.

- They serve as financial instruments of investment or trading.

What is cryptocurrency?

Cryptocurrency is a digital asset that is distributed in a vast network of computers. It has a decentralized structure that exists beyond the control and influence of central banking authorities or governments. Unlike the traditional or 'fiat' currencies like euros and dollars, cryptocurrencies only exist in the virtual domain. You know that you own them but you cannot see or hold them. You only have the numbers or the amounts in your digital account.

The term cryptocurrency comes from the concept of encryption technique that governs its operation. It is a complex system of cryptographic techniques and encryption algorithms that are similar to solving mathematical problems to secure and authenticate every transaction.

This highly sophisticated encryption process is also responsible for the production of new units of existing cryptocurrencies. Cryptocurrencies are developed by miners as codes. These special codes cannot be replicated by ordinary methods, making Bitcoin and Altcoins virtually safe against cyberattacks.

How does cryptocurrency work?

Cryptocurrency has changed people's shop, pay, or transact business. It allows users to send or receive coins as a form of payment for goods and services anywhere in the world.

Consumers, investors, and traders who like the convenience of cashless and hassle-free transactions prefer to use cryptocurrencies.

Blockchain Technology

The key technology behind cryptocurrencies is the blockchain. This distributed ledger technology (DLT) works as a database for all virtual transactions. Every single transaction is verified through 'consensus', a digital process that requires multiple systems to verify the authenticity of the algorithm output and create 'blocks.' All transactions require the unique signature of users.

Miners confirm the transactions. Their tasks involve accepting the transaction, stamping it as legit, and then sharing it in the network nodes. Each node will confirm its validity and add it to the database, becoming a permanent part of the blockchain.

Blockchain stores all the data in blocks after verification and then chained them together in chronological order.

The decentralized nature of this record-keeping technology makes all entries permanent, irreversible, and viewable by users. All the personal details are kept safe and immutable.

This incorruptible database works continuously and chronologically timestamps and records blocks or transactions. It operates using public-private key pairs, hash codes, and elliptical curve encryption.

- *Hash codes* – All blocks in the ledger system have their own hashes. They are created using a math function that converts the digital information or data gathered into a unique string of letters and numbers.

  Hashes verify the validity of information but do not necessarily reveal the details of the information.

  The hash code changes when someone attempts to change the information. For example, the hash is 68350abcde12345wxyz of a certain transaction and a hacker altered it by changing one character.

The other nodes will find it suspicious after cross-referencing with their own copies and cast away the version as invalid or illegitimate.

For hacking to be successful, the hacker needs to alter 51% of copies on the blockchain.

It would also require a lot of time, resources, and money to redo the hash codes and timestamps.

- *Public-private key pair* – They are digital keys that allow the encryption and decryption of the user's confidential information.

  The keys are secret strings of numbers and letters that you use to confirm your authority to use your bitcoin balance for any kind of crypto transaction.

- *Elliptic-curve cryptography (ECC)* – It is a public-key approach that secures the crypto account, ensuring that funds can be used only by the rightful owners. Bitcoin, Ethereum, and other crypto use the elliptic curve secp256k1 ($y^2 = x^3+7$ equation).

Peer-to-Peer System (P2P)

A peer-to-peer system is the core of Bitcoin and other cryptocurrencies. It uses a distributed network to make the exchange of coins or digital assets convenient, quick, and efficient. A P2P network consists of nodes or participants that perform similar tasks and have equal power. Every node is an individual peer that works by storing and sharing the files with other nodes.

The distributed architecture of the P2P system works independently and is more resistant to cyberattacks. There is no central server or intermediaries. It makes transferring Bitcoin or any other crypto worldwide quick and secure. Each node in the network has its own copy of the blockchain that it uses to compare with other nodes for data accuracy. Any inaccuracy or malicious activity is quickly denied by the system, making the requested transaction invalid.

How did cryptocurrency come into being?

The idea of using electronic money started in the '80s. The two countries that showed early interest to break into this revolutionary concept of using virtual currency were the Netherlands and the United States.

There were several attempts to introduce digital currency in the market but failed to gain traction.

- DigiCash was one of the noted attempts but eventually ceased from existence in the 1990s. It was created by David Chaum, a mathematician and computer scientist. Some people believe that he played a significant role in the later development of cryptocurrency.

- Paypal and other competitors emerged after that but used a hybrid approach by offering digital transactions with traditional currencies.

- Other attempts include Bit Gold, Hashcash, B-Money, and Flooz.

The idea of cryptocurrency was introduced in 1998 by Wei Dai, a computer engineer that developed the b-money cryptocurrency system and the Crypto + + cryptographic library. Dai also co-authored the proposal to use the VMAC message authentication algorithm. To honor his big contribution to cryptocurrencies and cryptography, the smallest sub-unit of Ether is named 'Wei'.

Wei Dai talked about cryptography and how it can be used to create or transact new forms of money, instead of relying on the central authorities.

When he published a paper about 'b-money,' the anonymous and distributed electronic cash system, Dai caught the interest of the public. The core concepts of b-money were later seen in the operations of Bitcoin and eventually in altcoins.

The breakthrough happened when Bitcoin was introduced by the mysterious Satoshi Nakamoto to the world in 2009. He referenced Wei Dai's b-money paper in his Bitcoin whitepaper and adopted most of the core concepts like:

- The need for a specific amount of computational work.
- The work done is updated and verified using a collective ledger book.
- The fund exchange is done by collective bookkeeping and authentication process that uses cryptographic hashes.
- The efforts of workers are awarded funds.
- The contract is enforced through the broadcast and uses digital signatures for transactions.

During the inception of Bitcoin in 2008, Nakamoto contacted Dai, He also discussed business with another cryptographer Adam Back who is behind Hashcash, the concept that is utilized by miners during Bitcoin mining.

Dai and Back were speculated to be "Satoshi Nakamoto". Both denied the rumors. Other 'suspects' include:

- Nick Szabo is a noted computer scientist and cryptographer famous for his digital currency and digital contract research papers.

- Hal Finney was the second developer of PGP Corporation and was one of the early contributors to Bitcoin. The 10 bitcoins he received from Yakamoto was recorded

Key Point

Cryptocurrency is an electronic currency that you can exchange for fiat currency like U.S. dollars or buy another cryptocurrency but is not recognize as legal tender.

The creation of new cryptocurrencies

Blockchain plays a central role in the creation of a new type of cryptocurrency. No one owns or controls this powerful technology, allowing anyone to create his own digital currency.

Satoshi Nakamoto has cleared the path by creating Bitcoin and many developers followed to exploit the innovative system. Charlie Lee, a former engineer of Google, helped the creators of Litecoin. All crypto creators aim to produce a better version of Bitcoin to mimic its traction and popularity.

There are 2 ways to create new cryptocurrencies:

1. By building a new blockchain

This option requires the coding skills of professionals and experts. To make new coins, the developer needs to choose a blockchain platform. The 10 popular platforms are Ethereum (with 82.70% market share), Waves, NEMNxt, MultiChain, BitShares 2.0, Hyperledger Fabric, Blockstarter, IBM blockchain, CoinList, and EOS.

The work begins by designing the nodes. The nodes support the blockchain and are responsible for data storage, verification, and processing of transactions. Blockchains need nodes to ensure efficiency and utmost security.

After the nodes are built, the developer will work to establish the internal architecture of the new blockchain. The features include Address Formats, Permissions, Key Formats, Asset Issuance, Asset Reissuance, Key Management, Parameters, Atomic Swaps, Native Assets, MultiSignatures, Block Signatures, and Hand-shaking.

Once done with the architecture, the developer needs to check the Application Programming Interface (API) that is already provided by the blockchain platform. Then, proceed in designing the Admin and User Interface.

2. By modifying the existing process to form a new 'fork' or variant

Most of the Altcoins are forks or variants of the Bitcoin protocol like LitecoinBitcoin, GoldMain, and CashBitcoin. Garlicoin is forked from Litecoin.

Forking an existing blockchain involves taking an open-source code, making some changes, then launching the new blockchain with a brand new name.

This requires skills to know the sections of the codes to modify. Changing the parameters of the blockchain or introducing new features necessitates creating a 'fork.'

A 'fork' is technically an updated software, where all full nodes or participants are running the same software to access the blockchain. This ensures network security and convenience to verify the transactions.

There are two kinds of forks:

- A **hard fork** requires the developer to update the software by 90-95% because the nodes of the non-updated version can no longer access the system.

- A **soft fork** refers to the majority of nodes that need modification to update existing software while allowing the previous version to continue working.

There are two ways to generate a fork. One is using a fork coin generator like ForkGen. It works for people who are not equipped with programming skills.

The other option is to do it yourself by searching in Github, downloading, compiling the code, reconfiguring, implementing customization, and publishing the code back to Github.

The final step is to create a white paper or documentation and share it via a dedicated website.

As of May 2021, there are more than 10,000 kinds of cryptocurrency in existence. Each of them has its own unique properties and functionalities that leverage blockchain technology in the fields of finance, health, energy, supply and logistics, data storage, privacy and security, content ownership, social networks, and more.

Cryptocurrencies function as:

- Currency

  Bitcoin and the majority of the cryptocurrencies have store value and can be used as a retail payment like the traditional fiats.

- Platform or app

  Some cryptocurrencies function as platform or app crypto. Augur, for instance, is used to launch the Ethereum network.

- Utility

  The group of crypto with utility functions is developed as infrastructure, allowing other cryptocurrencies to be built on top of them. Ethereum has the Ethereum Virtual Machine that allows the creation of token coins.

Technically, cryptocurrencies are secured by solid cryptography, not by trust or people.

The consensus-keeping process enhanced their monetary and transactional properties.

Transactional properties

- Anonymity – Crypto accounts and transactions do not impose a connection to the real-world identities of the users. The addresses are created using minimum personal data and the blockchain does not reveal details, only the flow transactions.

- Global and fast – Instant propagation and confirmation of transactions within seconds. The virtual network is indifferent to geographical locations and borders.

- No gatekeeper – As long as you have downloaded the software and a crypto wallet for your coins or tokens, you can start using them to pay for goods and services or trade with other investors.

- Irreversible – Once transactions are confirmed, they cannot be undone or reversed by anyone including the senders. Nobody can help you retrieve your coins if you send them to a fraudulent receiver.

- Secure – The solid cryptography system locks all crypto funds. All users have private keys to access their own assets.

Monetary properties

- Controlled and limited supply – Bitcoin has a cap that is expected to happen around the year 2140. Most altcoins do not have a limit cap but follow the schedule written in their codes to create new coins and tokens.

- Representation of itself- Cryptocurrencies represent themselves, not numbers or debts like the Fiat currencies. Bitcoin and altcoins are bearers of their own values and follow their proprietary systems.

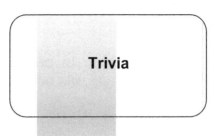

Trivia

Some of the celebrities who invested in crypto are Floyd Mayweather, Gwyneth Paltrow, Elon Musk, Snoop Dogg, Paris Hilton, 50 Cent, and Rapper Logic.

Mining: The method of creating new coins of existing cryptocurrencies

The only way to produce new units or more crypto coins is through mining. This process involves solving cryptographic puzzles or complex mathematical problems.

Mining requires great computing power and is very competitive. In Bitcoin, the SHA 256 Hash algorithm sets the basis of the cryptologic puzzle.

The first miner who solves the puzzle can build and add a block to the blockchain. As an incentive, he will receive a certain number of coins or tokens.

To ensure that no peer can break the stability of the blockchain, the puzzles become more difficult over time and require the miners to invest more computer power to successfully create new cryptocurrencies.

Bitcoin has a maximum cap of coins while alternative coins (altcoins) limit the available coins in circulation each year but do not have a maximum number of target coins.

Anyone with the knowledge and skills can be a crypto miner. But because there is no central authority to delegate the task, Satoshi requires that all interested miners find the 'hash', which is a cryptographic function product that connects the newly mined block with the existing blocks in the network. It is referred to as 'Proof-of-Work.'

The rationale of this rule is to prevent the breakdown of the cryptocurrency network due to forged transactions created by abusive parties.

Are crypto coins and tokens the same?

While coins and tokens are both cryptocurrencies, they are different from each other. Depending on the given crypto codes, miners can generate not just new coins for existing cryptocurrencies but also tokens.

- Coins have independent transaction ledgers while tokens are dependent on the underlying network to validate and secure the transactions or ownerships.

- Coins need their own blockchains while tokens operate on the existing blockchains.

- Coins can be used anywhere and for any purpose, while tokens are limited to certain projects only.

- Coins can buy tokens while tokens cannot be used to purchase coins.

- Coins are instruments to transfer wealth possession, tokens only represent a 'contract' (loyalty points, event tickets, physical/tangible objects).

Tokens are usually released through ICO or initial coin offering, which is also called a 'token launch' or a 'token sale.'

This crowd selling technique can be used for raising proceeds to create a product or building a consumer base of early birds to get the offered product. Many companies use ICO because it bypasses the banks' or venture capitalists' regulated capital-raising process. And even if a particular ICO ended, interested people can buy the publicly available tokens using the underlying currency.

Is cryptocurrency secure and safe to use?

Technically, the purpose of encryption is to provide ultimate safety and security to all digital transactions. This advanced coding transmits and stores the data between the users' electronic wallets and blockchains. These public ledgers are hard to tamper or hack, making them more secure.

Moreover, all transactions need users to use a 2-factor authentication process like entering a username and a password. You also need to enter the authentication code that you will receive in your mobile phone messaging system.

But remember that just because securities are high doesn't mean that they are unhackable. History shows that Bitcoin and other cryptocurrencies are subject to online thefts and hacking.

In 2018, the crypto world was rocked when Coincheck and BitGrail were hacked to the tune of $534 million and $195 million respectively. While blockchains are very secure, the other aspects of the crypto ecosystem like wallets and exchange platforms are not immune from scammers and hackers.

Where to store your crypto coins?

You need a 'digital wallet' to buy cryptocurrencies. This kind of wallet is an online app that stores your coins. It acts like a digital bank account that you can open using your private key.

The digital wallet you will need also depends on the kind of crypto you like to possess. If you want Litecoin, find one that stores this coin. If you like Bitcoin, choose a wallet that safely stores bitcoins. It is important to find a secure cryptocurrency wallet to prevent possible theft. Once your coins are stolen, there is no way to get them back again.

2 general types of crypto wallets:

Hot wallet (software)

A hot wallet is easy to set up, but the least safe among the three options. It runs on phones, tablets, computers, or any internet-connected device which makes this type of wallet vulnerable to hackers. It generates your private keys so you can access your coins. So, while it is very convenient to use during transactions, storing the private key on the device makes it prone to hacking.

To avoid possible security and privacy threats, it is crucial to use tighter security such as two-factor authentication, strong password, or safe browsing on the internet. Also, use this wallet for small spending or transactions only.

Cold wallet (hardware)

A cold wallet or hardware wallet is a portable device that you can connect to your laptop or computer via USB. It is the safer option because it stores your cryptocurrency in offline mode. This type of wallet is like a treasure vault that keeps your funds secure when you are not doing transactions or trading activities. Some cold wallets require the internet to connect, while others do not need it.

Under these two categories are 4 types of crypto wallets:

- **Web or Online wallet**

  This wallet allows you to access your Bitcoin fund via a web browser. While it is the quickest option to complete your transaction, it is vulnerable to unauthorized attempts and cyber threats. It is best not to store all your bitcoins in this kind of wallet.

- **Desktop wallet**

A desktop wallet is an example of a cold wallet or cold storage. It allows you to store your bitcoins privately and securely, but make sure to use ultimate security especially if you need to use an internet connection to make transactions.

- **Mobile wallet**

A mobile wallet is a downloadable app that is installed on your phone or other mobile devices. It is internet-based, which is risky. What is nice about this thing is you can easily scan your mobile wallet's QR code to complete your purchases.

- **Paper wallet**

It is another offline storage that requires generating private and public keys, then printing them on paper. The generated code or information on that piece of paper lets you access your digital address, so make sure to keep it safe. Paper wallets are best for long-term and high-security kinds of investment, not for traders or constant users.

Ways to acquire crypto coins

Cryptocurrencies are available in exchange platforms and brokers who facilitate the buying and selling between investors/traders and the market. They can be bought using fiat currencies and cryptocurrencies (whichever is preferred by the sellers).

To start buying cryptocurrencies, you need to download a digital wallet. A lot of exchange platforms have built-in wallets, but it is up to you to have a separate crypto wallet for your coins and tokens.

Exchange versus brokers

Crypto exchange is an online platform where buyers and sellers directly trade coins and tokens. Using an exchange is the traditional way of trading crypto. It allows people to trade crypto for both crypto and fiat currencies.

It is ideal for both beginners and advanced users who like to speculate on the prices.

The most popular and trusted exchanges where you can buy altcoins are Binance, Coinbase, CEX.io, Bitfinex, Gemini, FTX, Changelly, KuCoin, Huobi Global, Bittrex, Coinmama, Bitstamp, and Kraken.

- **Binance** offers the widest variety of alternative coins and supports over 500 trading pairs. It is best for traders who want a diverse altcoin portfolio and trade their crypto against Bitcoin pairs. It accepts fiat currencies as payment for crypto coins and tokens.

- **CEX.io** is a very secure exchange that also works as a trading exchange. If you are planning to buy or sell Bitcoin, DASH, and Ethereum, it is the best place to invest in crypto. It accepts EUR, USD, RUB, and GBP currencies as well as bank transfer and debit/credit cards. Card fees are around 3.5% plus $0.20.

- **Coinmama** is one of the highly trusted and easiest to use crypto exchanges. It offers Ether and Bitcoin to investors and traders from almost all countries in the world. Coinmama accepts local currency and credit cards for payments. However, it charges a 6% fee to cards which is higher than the others.

- **Gemini** has Bitcoin, Ether, Litecoin, Zcash, and other altcoins. This U.S-based exchange charges $0.99 to 1.49% transaction fees and a fee of 0.5%.

- **Bitstamp** has more options to choose from, including Bitcoin, Bitcoin Cash, Litecoin, Ripple, and Ether. You can pay through your credit/debit cards, bank transfer, Euro, or U.S. dollars. It is a bit more complicated to use, so this is best for advanced traders.

  It is recommended to buy big amounts when you use a credit card because it charges exorbitant fees for small purchases. If you use a debit card, you will be charged $10 if your deposit is below $1,000 and 2% for more than $1,000 deposit.

A crypto broker is either a person or a firm that provides financial services for people who buy or sell their cryptocurrencies. Brokers charge users the use of their platforms. Some platforms like Bitpanda can be both an exchange and a broker.

The best crypto brokers include Coinbase, Kriptomart, eToro, Robinhood, and TradeStation,

- **Coinbase** has a variety of altcoin choices, including Ethereum, Litecoin, DAI, DASH, EOS, and Ripples.

It is the U.S. biggest broker exchange and is available in Europe, North America, and Australia. If you live in South America, Africa, and Asia, you cannot buy crypto from Coinbase. It charges 0.50% when you buy or sell crypto below $10,000 in value and less as the order becomes higher.

- **Kriptomat** was established in 2019 and is considered one of the safest and simplest brokerages to buy cryptocurrencies. It will only take 5 minutes to upload the required documents and start trading Ether or Bitcoin with this platform.

  Kriptomat has great customer support and is available in 21 languages. The buying/selling fees are only 1.45%. It does not charge extra fees whenever you transfer or withdraw cryptocurrencies.

- **Robinhood** is a mainstream investment broker that facilitates buying and selling of crypto. Its user-friendly platform is secure and ideal for new crypto users who want to invest in a variety of strong altcoins.

  It has wider payment methods and allows users to withdraw funds from their external accounts. It has no purchase fee but charges an order flow fee.

Other buying options:

Bitcoin ATMs

These ATMs work like the traditional machines, but the difference is you will be depositing your cash to buy coins rather than withdrawing money. This is the quickest way to own bitcoins, but be ready to pay 5-10% transaction fees.

To use a Bitcoin ATM, find one and verify your identity. It may require your phone number to send the code. Once you receive it, enter the code and your digital wallet address.

Then, deposit your cash into the machine to enable it to send your purchased coins to your crypto wallet. Wait for your receipt and you're done.

Peer-to-Peer (P2P)

Another cool way to buy cryptocurrencies is P2P because it is direct and does not use a middleman. For this method, you need to find a P2P website and create your account. It is free and simple. For Bitcoin, you can go to LocalBitcoins and if you want Ether, look for Localtherum.com.

The next step is to check the listing of cryptocurrencies and their prices. Check the price that sellers set for their cryptocurrencies.

Find the best available payment option for you.

Don't forget to check the customers' reviews about the seller before making a decision. Once you have chosen one, enter your details that are asked for like:

- Amount or how much is your budget

- Currency or the option you want to pay with

- Payment method

Some sellers or buyers would ask for valid identification, so be ready to send a photo of your ID, a scanned image of your driver's license or passport, or a selfie while holding the document.

Once the trader accepts your request, you will receive the amount of coin in the website's escrow. Then the seller will send you a reference number that you will use to send the payment.

The advantages of using P2P are there are no fees and you can use cash to pay for them. But you need to be extremely careful when selecting sellers.

Other ways to earn cryptocurrencies other than buying:

Mining crypto

For this option, you need to use your computer skills to solve mathematical equations to obtain coins. It will also require a high-end computer model with Application-Specific Integrated Circuit because regular computers do not work for mining. So, that means investing thousands of dollars in the equipment.

If you don't want to spend a lot of money, another option is to work with other miners by joining a mining network.

Staking

Stalking or Proof of Stake system where people are chosen for the number of coins they are holding. The more you hold and place into staking, the more opportunity for you to be chosen to confirm new block creation.

Promoting projects through micro tasks

Find companies and startups that offer crypto coins as rewards or bounties for completing tasks like:

- Writing press releases

- Making video reviews

- Distributing promotional videos

- Writing testimonials

Taking advantage of project campaigns through airdrops

Many companies are using airdrop campaigns to build a community or initial traction in exchange for tokens. These tokens can be sold or traded for crypto coins or cash when the project takes off.

The tasks include:

- Sharing posts

- Following the companies' social media platforms

- Downloading the apps

- Completing forms about the project

- Signing up on the platforms

DeFi Yield Farming

Decentralized Finance Yield Farming, also known as liquidity mining, is a reward system that works like a bond market.

To gain interest and rewards, you need to lock in your cryptocurrency. Aside from the yield you harvest, you can also earn additional tokens depending on the projects that you choose. The popular DeFis are Compound (COMP), Ren (REN), Kyber Network (KNC), and Ox (ZRX).

Accepting crypto payments

If you have an e-commerce website in WooCommerce or Shopify, start accepting cryptocurrencies as a payment option.

Get paid in cryptocurrency by freelancing

Look for platforms that offer freelancing jobs and pay cryptocurrency. You can check Cryptocurrenjobs or Ethlance.

Joining publishers' network

Earn crypto coins by joining crypto publishers' networks and get paid for displaying ads of various companies.

Earning coins from crypto faucets

The faucet system works by simply watching ads, playing games, or completing surveys to earn Satoshis (unit of Bitcoin) or Wei (unit of Ethereum).

When your coins reach the minimum amount, you can withdraw your earnings and cash them out.

Earning cashback

Digital banking is becoming more innovative now, offering opportunities for users to earn crypto by depositing funds or spending using cards to earn cashback.

Gambling your crypto bonus

There are crypto gambling platforms that give a login bonus in crypto. Use the bonus to double up or multiple your funds.

However, the platforms require a minimum deposit before you can withdraw the coins

When choosing a cryptocurrency exchange or broker, look for the following:

- **Security**

  You need to check the background and reputation of the company behind the exchange. If the history shows that it has been hacked before, consider it as a red flag and check the others.

- **Quick verification**

  Is it easy to create an account and get verified?

- **Transaction fee**

  The lower the transaction fees, the better for you.

- **Payment options**

  An exchange that accepts more payment options makes trading more convenient.

- **Cryptocurrency listing**

  If you like different coins, choose a broker exchange that offers more than one type of cryptocurrency.

- **Users reviews**

The customer reviews help you know the exchange better.

<u>FAQs</u>

What is the difference between cryptocurrencies and digital currencies?

Cryptocurrencies exist across the network of computers and are not issued by the central banks or governments. Digital currencies also exist in the virtual world but are issued by the central authorities and possess the characteristics of fiat or traditional currencies.

Why are the reasons why cryptocurrencies are the subject of criticism?

Some of these reasons are the vulnerability of the underlying infrastructure, volatility of exchange rate, and use for illegal activities like tax evasion or money laundering.

What are the advantages of cryptocurrency?

They are being praised for transparency, inflation resistance, portability, and divisibility.

Their anonymity nature is also beneficial for people and companies that value their privacy and security above all.

How secure are crypto transfers between users?

Cryptocurrency uses keys (public keys and private keys) to secure the fund transfers from one user to another user. The public key is used to transfer funds to the account address or crypto wallet, while the private key is the owner's 'code' or 'pin' to sign transactions.

Do cryptocurrencies represent a currency, cash, or cash equivalent?

They are not legal tender and lack the backup of any government or legal entity, so cryptocurrencies are not foreign currencies, cash equivalent, or cash. Cryptocurrencies are digital alternatives to traditional money that are primarily used by investors and traders for speculating the rise or fall of assets' value.

Is cryptocurrency a good investment?

Investing in cryptocurrency involves risks and is not for the faint-hearted. However, it also offers lots of potential benefits and financial rewards.

What are the Pros and Cons of investing in crypto?

- *Pros*
  High return potential
  Diversification

- *Cons*
  Greater volatility
  Potential for fraud and scams
  No benchmark for valuation

Will I go rich in trading cryptocurrency?

Crypto trading is just one way to maximize the potential of your coins. Trading however is the quickest and the easiest way to multiply your cryptocurrency. But it is also the fastest way to lose all your crypto.

Are cryptocurrencies taxed?

The 2014 IRS ruling in the United States of America defines virtual currencies like crypto as property. It means that whenever you use cryptocurrency to purchase something, it will be subjected to capital gain tax rules. To avoid tax evasion charges, traders should disclose their crypto transactions to the IRS.

It includes:

- Payment for products or services
- Cashing out or exchanging crypto coins for fiat currency
- Receiving forked or mined coins
- Exchanging crypto for another crypto

The non-taxable activities are:

- Purchasing crypto using fiat money
- Transfer cryptocurrency from one wallet to another digital wallet
- Sending crypto as a gift to third parties
- Donating cryptocurrency to charity or any tax-exempt non-profit organization

Is cryptocurrency legal?

Cryptocurrencies are legal in the United States and some other parts of the world. China, on the other hand, bans its usage. Other countries that restrict the use of cryptocurrencies are Saudi Arabia, Mexico, Egypt, and Zambia. It is illegal in Bangladesh, while users can go to jail when crypto is used in Nepal, Vietnam, Algeria, Ecuador, Bolivia, and Morocco. Ultimately, the legality of crypto depends on the country or state.

Chapter 2

Beginners Guide in Cryptocurrency Trading

The most obvious way to make money out of your cryptocurrency is to engage in trading. If you do it right, crypto trading will give you tremendous returns compared to traditional investments. In just a short period, you can be a millionaire or multi-millionaire, or a loser in the trading sphere.

This high volatility and growth potential of crypto makes it very attractive to investors and traders who want to multiply their money. It is common for crypto coin prices to display exponential growth or fluctuate more than 10%. Interest in cryptocurrency has been increasing.

Many traditional investors and millennials are diversifying their investment portfolio, adding bitcoins and altcoins as investment and trading instruments.

At a glance

- ✓ **Trading vs. Investing**
- ✓ **Top benefits of crypto trading**
- ✓ **How does crypto trading differ from other trading options?**
- ✓ **Different kinds of trading styles**
- ✓ **How to pick the right trading style?**
- ✓ **Elements that affect crypto trading**
- ✓ **Basic steps in crypto trading**
- ✓ **Two approaches in crypto trading**
- ✓ **Things to remember before trading your crypto**
- ✓ **Frequently Asked Questions (FAQs)**

Trading vs. Investing

Trading and investing are two economic concepts that involve buying assets to grow wealth by earning profits. In the financial markets, assets are called instruments. They come in the form of bonds, stocks, cryptocurrency, options, margin products, currency pairs (Forex market), and many others.

Trading

As a newbie who wants to delve into the exciting cryptocurrency sphere, your first step is to understand what crypto trading is all about and how to be a successful trader. You need to create a game plan and follow the clearly defined steps to achieve your trading goals. Basically, trading is the term for short-term trading because it involves active positioning (enter and exit) in short period frames.

But trading is more than that as it uses different types of strategies like trend trading, day trading, swing trading, and more. When you trade your cryptocurrencies, you speculate on the price movements by buying or selling the coins via a broker exchange or contracts for difference (CFDs) trading account.

Investing

Investing refers to allocating resources or money to buy a property, asset, or financial instrument and selling it in the future at a higher amount. The core of investment is the ROI or return on investment. Unlike trading, investing involves waiting for a longer period like years or decades before selling the asset.

The main objective of investing is building wealth over a certain time which usually takes a decade or more. It is more of a passive approach where investors are not concerned about the price fluctuations.

While both seek to gain profits, the traders and investors use different methods to achieve their financial goals.

- Traders are constantly watching the market trends and taking advantage of its volatility. If you are into trading, you need to enter and exit positions to gain returns.

- Investors wait for a time being to get their target ROI for their investments, which typically are double or larger than the amount they spend to buy the asset.

Trivia

The business value that is added by blockchain would surpass $3.1 trillion by 2030.

Top benefits of cryptocurrency trading

- **Volatility**

    The volatility element of cryptocurrency makes it more exciting to trade and invest. Its rapid price movements in a single day allow traders to go short or long. These two jargons represent the core of trading. Both reflect the possible direction of the cryptocurrency- either to rise in value or fall.

    When you go "long" or buy a cryptocurrency, you are hoping that you will generate a profit from a certain point. In contrast, when you go "short", you sell your cryptocurrency because you are expecting that its price will fall from a certain point.

- **Ability to go short or long**

    When you trade, your primary aim is to see your asset increase in value. So, during trading, you should always take advantage of the rising and falling of crypto prices.

- **Availability**

Because of the decentralized nature of cryptocurrency, the market is open for trading 24/7. You can trade whenever you want or make direct transactions with other users via crypto exchanges anywhere in the world. However, there are times when the crypto market is unavailable due to 'forks' or infrastructural updates.

- **Anonymity and privacy**

If you use decentralized crypto exchanges, you can trade without identifying yourself. While in a centralized trading platform, you share some of your particulars but remain anonymous to other traders.

- **Quick account opening**

Before you can start trading cryptocurrency, you need to open and register your exchange account. For this purpose, you need to find a trusted broker exchange that offers a simple registration form and quick verification.

Creating an account is a breeze and you can begin trading right away.

• **Multitude of assets**

The cryptocurrency market, despite being new, has given traders easy access to CFDs, leveraged tokens, futures, options, swaps, and other stock market products.

• **Leveraged exposure**

Opting for CFD or contract for difference gives you leveraged exposure. CFD allows you to go short or go long and trade on margin. It is also used by investors to hedge their physical portfolios. This leveraged product lets you buy a small percentage to trade on margin or open a position.

When trading CFDs, you do not buy or sell the entire commodity, physical share, currency pair, stock index, or any underlying asset, just units you believe will give you profits as their prices go up or down. When the price moves upward, you will be gaining a lot based on the units you sold or bought.

The opposite will entail losses. Your profits and losses depend on the size of your position.

Other advantages of buying CFD are:

- It leverages your market position by trading a fraction upfront.

- It lets you speculate and trade without owning the whole range of assets.

- It gives you the option to trade on more than one exchange.

- It does not impose paying fees when depositing or withdrawing crypto.

How does crypto trading differ from other trading options?

Trading involves a risk, but cryptocurrency is often viewed as riskier compared to other types of traditional trading. To know the risks involved, let me make some comparisons and help you weigh the pros and cons.

Crypto trading vs Stock trading

The market in crypto trading is based on supply and demand, making it highly speculative. The value of the digital coin is dependent on what the investors pay to own it.

There is also a finite supply, making it scarce. The scarcity drives the price upward and gives you lucrative gains. In addition, the crypto market is working 24/7 and reacts to outside events that can double your profits.

In contrast, stock trading is more stable, offering returns of investments for a longer period. Most of the companies offering stocks will remain in the future, so stockholders gain passive income. The stock trading market works in a conventional way, with public holidays and weekends.

Similarities:

- Investing and trading tools are almost similar- Traders of stocks and cryptocurrency use charts and perform Technical Analysis (TA).

- Investing and trading strategies are the same – Stock traders and crypto traders use swing, position, or day trading styles. They can also choose to buy and hold financial assets.

- Use similar market products – Innovative products in stock trading like derivatives, options, futures, and leveraged tokens can now be traded in the crypto market. Crypto traders also utilize stock trading techniques like leveraging to inflate gains.

Differences

- Market volatility – The stock market is less volatile and offers better stability. In contrast, the crypto market is characterized by wild price swings.

- Market assets – In the cryptocurrency market, you are investing your wealth in the currency or token, the technology, or the idea. While in the stock market, you buy shares of stocks from publicly listed companies.

- Market maturity – The trade volume and market value of the stock market is larger compared to the cryptocurrency market because it has been existing for a longer period. The crypto market is just over a decade old which contributes to its wild volatility.

- Regulations-The stock market is governed by rules and regulations, while the cryptocurrency market is deregulated and does not conform to any rule or regulations of the central authority or government.

Crypto trading vs Forex trading

Both involve currency trading. Their prices are influenced by supply and demand in the market. Trading requires knowledge and familiarity with how the market operates and behaves.

Crypto traders buy or sell Bitcoin or any kind of Altcoin and use them as instruments to make profits. To maximize the potential of your crypto, you should have a solid trading strategy, a good understanding of the exchange market, and risk management techniques.

Forex or foreign exchange market involves buying and selling of currencies. Traders know that by trading in this world's largest financial market, they will be benefiting a lot. Some of these advantages include:

- 23 hours trading during the week
- wide choices of available currencies
- low transaction costs
- volatility

Forex is time-sensitive and good for short-term profits, while cryptocurrency does not guarantee when and how much is the potential pay-off until the market displays the positive signs.

Generally speaking, cryptocurrency trading has a higher potential for bigger returns while forex is more stable, regulated, and protected.

> **Key Point**
>
> *Avoid slippage risk by trading in low volatile markets or when the market activity is at its peak hours.*

Different kinds of active trading styles

Trading strategies guide traders when positioning in the crypto market. They depend on the traders' profile, goals, risk tolerances, and preferences.

Technically, they encompass what you are trading, the approach you are going to use to trade it, and the points of entry/exit.

Scalping, swing trading, day trading, and position trading are **active trading strategies**. These styles of trading work by identifying or timing favorable positions to 'beat the market average' for a short-term period.

1 - Day trading

Day trading refers to the strategy that allows traders to enter and exit positions during the same day or 24 hours. It requires quick decisions and execution, which can be stressful but exciting at the same time. It demands an extended period of watching your computer screen to monitor the price movements and take advantage of favorable positions.

Day traders keep their positions open within set periods and not beyond them. In this trading style, you have to rely often on technical analysis and chart patterns to know which kind of crypto to trade. You should also remember that in this type of trading, your profits can be minimal. But if you are very active, day trading is highly profitable.

Generally, it suits the well-experienced crypto traders or market-makers but beginners can learn by trading carefully. Moreover, the introduction of electronic trading makes it easy for novice traders.

The best cryptocurrencies for day trading are Ethereum (ETH), Tether (USDT), Binance Coin (BNB), EOS, and Tron (TRX).

2- Scalping

Scalping has the shortest time frames, requiring traders to enter and exit their positions within seconds or minutes to make the most of small price fluctuations. During these short time frames, traders earn small profits or lower than 1% percentage of profit that adds up over a longer time. But the goal here is to ensure constant profits and cut losses quickly. This type of active trading employs identifying and exploiting small moves frequently.

However, scalping is not recommended for beginners because it requires a lot of practice and understanding of how prices move in the crypto markets. To get the most of scalping, you need to watch out for short-term fluctuations and trade several positions every few minutes. You can also do spot buying and selling cryptocurrency. It necessitates constant focus and risk management by making short or long positions. It is also crucial where to use stops.

3- Swing trading

Swing trading has a longer time horizon which means you can hold your position from days to weeks. This means you can watch your position go up or down or HODL your position until you reach the next resistance level, hit your target, or meet a favorable exit condition.

Traders who use this style of trading typically buy or sell their coins as soon as the volatility occurs. They make trading rules or algorithms of their own based on fundamental analysis or technical analysis.

4- Position trading

Position trading, also called trend trading, works by purchasing assets and holding them for extended periods like months. The goal is to sell the assets in the future at a higher amount. It is ideal for beginners because the long time frames provide ample opportunity to weigh their decisions. For novices, it is regarded as a buy-and-hold trading style.

Position traders are on the lookout for trends to gain profits with the help of fundamental analysis. You need to take or build a short position high or long position low and stay with it for some time.

It looks like investing but the objective is to create a killer trade by acting on trends. By jumping or riding the 'wave', position traders benefit. They would exit quickly once the advantageous trend breaks.

Other styles of crypto trading:

Intraday trading

This is a type of day trading that lets the traders hold their positions multiple times throughout the regular trading hours. Take note that crypto markets do not really close, so the trading continues. You can use software that allows intraday traders to automate positions in the trading market.

Range trading

Range trading aims to trade the range, not to buy assets after a downtrend or buy during an uptrend. Range traders take advantage of the current range of predictable or profitable trades. They set stops to buy the range's bottom and then scale it out to the top and sell.

In this style of trading, the range provides a clear picture of support and resistance and works well when you use candlestick chart analysis.

The assumption is that the support and resistance hold the edges of the trading range until it breaks. In a simple explanation, it means the upper edge can push the current price downward, while the range's lower edge can push the crypto price upward.

When the price of the cryptocurrency ranges between the levels of support and resistance, you buy the support level/ exit at the support level and sell the resistance level/short the resistance level.

This straightforward style of trading is perfect for beginners, but you need to fully understand the concepts of support and resistance levels, candlestick charts, and momentum indicators such as Relative Strength Index Indicator (RSI) and Moving Average Convergence Divergence (MACD). Both are tools for Technical Analysis.

HFT or High-Frequency trading

High-frequency trading uses trading bots and algorithms for quick entry/exit in multiple positions within short time frames. HFT traders are likely to gain a significant advantage over competitors by taking advantage of a few milliseconds. This style is suitable for veteran traders.

It is popular among the 'quant' (or quantitative) traders who develop algorithms to execute complex strategies. While it may look like a day trading method, HFT is more complicated because it involves backtesting, keeping track, and tweaking the algorithms to match the constant changes in the market conditions. So while the trading bots make it easy for traders, traders are strategizing.

Moreover, developing your own HFT bots necessitated advanced knowledge of the market concepts, computer science, and mathematics. The other option is to buy an HFT bot.

How to pick the right trading style?

There is no right or wrong trading style. It all depends on the individual goals and preferences. Here are some general reminders that may help you during the selection.

- Find your trading style and refine it. You can calibrate your style as you practice your trading skills. Your goal here is to master your methodology by sticking to it. Do not change your style when it does not for some trading session or you feel that it is not delivering your targets, instead review and adjust your strategies.

- Expect failures, miscalculations, and mistakes when you are trading assets, especially cryptocurrency because of its volatility. The bull market does not stay easy or favorable to many traders, so always be prepared for some heartbreaks and financial loss. Learn the lessons and review your errors.

- Apply risk management protocols to reduce loss. This includes not switching from one style to another trading style. Adjust your strategy to have greater opportunities to gain profits.

  Do not be afraid to engage in the next trading because statistics show that the next trade can be your ticket to success.

- Take care of your crypto portfolio by avoiding buying high and selling low like the day trading at a low or investing at high. Understand how the market conditions move and learn the trading tricks. Take your time and do not attempt to do frenzy trading to prevent killing your portfolio.

Elements that affect cryptocurrency trading

As a newbie in crypto trading, you need to understand the following factors:

- **Market cap**

    Market cap or market capitalization in cryptocurrency refers to the value of all mined coins. The total value is determined by multiplying the number of coins that are circulating in the market by the present market price of the coin.

    ```
    Circulating Supply of Coin x Current Price

    = Market Cap
    ```

    So, if the circulating supply is 20,000,000 coins and the current price of the coin per unit is $10, the market cap of the particular crypto is $200,000,000.

The market cap also serves as an indicator to measure and monitor the market value of Bitcoin or Altcoins. It provides insight into the level of risk of the digital asset you have chosen and shows its growth potential. However, you need to remember that the market cap does not represent the money inflow or the amount of money in the crypto market. It is common for the cryptocurrency to jump its price and command a higher amount due to liquidity and volume.

Coins with small market caps are vulnerable to big holders' manipulation, causing wild price springs. High market cap coins are less vulnerable to wild volatility and manipulation.

- **Trading volume**

The trading volume shows the amount of traded individual units at a given time. In the cryptocurrency market, it is the quintessential factor and essential technical indicator. By using it when trading crypto, traders easily measure how strong the underlying trend is.

Coins with higher trading volume are easier to buy or sell, while low trading volume indicates a lack of liquidity. Cryptocurrencies that show very low trading volume is a sign of a declining or ailing trading volume.

The presence of high trading volume and high volatility are leading signs that there will be a massive price movement (win or loss). This means that a lot of investors and traders are active in the market during that price level. It is the best time for traders to make an entry or exit move. Volatility without a high volume marker is an indication of a weak trend.

• Stop-loss orders and stop-limit orders

A stop-loss order is the market order or limit that is activated when the asset reaches a certain price point or the stop price. Its main purpose is to limit the trader's loss and avoid wiping out his wealth. It works by setting your stop price that will invalidate your order or loss during the trading.

The stop-limit refers to buying or selling cryptocurrency at a certain amount or better. This limit-buy order is triggered when your order reaches the limit price or lower price. The limit-sell order is executed when the limit price is reached or higher.

You need to understand the stop-loss can be a stop-market order or a stop-limit order. While they vary, you can use them both if you want. However, you need to remember that the stop-limit order is only fulfilled when it reaches the validation point or better, but not when the market crashes down.

If your stop-loss is the same as your stop-loss when the price drops, it will move away from the set price and leave the order unfulfilled. To make sure that you can exit the market when you reach the limit during these extreme conditions, opt for the stop-market order.

- **Storage**

Knowing where and how to store your cryptocurrency is another important factor when you are into trading, especially when it involves a huge amount. The rule of the thumb is to set aside a trading fund that you will willingly lose when things get worse. Never use your savings or other investments for trading purposes, whether it involves crypto or traditional assets.

Finding a trusted broker exchange is also crucial because your investment will be under their custody, making it risky and less secure against scammers. To ensure total control and security over your digital assets, it is best to store them on hardware wallets.

Another option is choosing a trustworthy software wallet that you can easily access from your smartphone, laptop, iPad, or desktop by using your private key. However, since the transactions involve internet connectivity, you need to have tighter security to prevent online thefts or hacking.

Basic steps in cryptocurrency trading

Step 1: Choose a crypto brokerage or exchange

Like fiat trading, you need a place where cryptocurrencies are traded.

Every crypto exchange has its terms of service and way of trading. Among the popular exchanges are Coinbase, Binance, Bitstamp, Bitfinex, CEX.io, Coinmama, eToro, GeminiKriptomat, and KuCoin.

For beginners, it is best to choose an exchange that offers a variety of crypto coins and has a user-friendly interface. Some exchanges do not accept fiat currency as payment, so you have to purchase a crypto coin first to buy coins.

Step 2: Create an account

To register as a user and start trading, you need to make an account. It will require providing personal information like your date of birth, email address, home address, and Social Security number.

Step 3: Select a crypto wallet

You can choose to store your crypto in software or hardware wallets. Between the two, the hardware is more secure because it is a physical device that you can plug into your computer and use offline.

For software wallets, there are several free options on Android, iOS, and Google Chrome. Most cryptocurrencies come with official wallets like Bitcoin Core Wallet, MyEtherWallet or Ethereum Wallet, Dash Core, or Litecoin-QT. Exchanges and brokerages have also built-in wallets like Coinbase and Poloniex.

You can also find multi-currency wallets if you want to invest/trade using various types of crypto coins. Some examples are:

- Coinomi allows you to transact with 64 cryptocurrencies

- Jaxx Wallet supports Bitcoin, Bitcoin Cash Ethereum, Dash, Litecoin, Ethereum Classic, Zcash, and more

- Exodus can be used for sending and storing Bitcoin, Bitcoin Cash, Litecoin, Ethereum Classic, Ethereum, etcetera

Step 4: Fund your crypto account or wallet

Once your account in a crypto brokerage is approved, you can fund it by connecting to your bank account. You have the option to use wire transfer or debit cards.

Step 5: **Pick your cryptocurrency**

Before buying, compare the different cryptocurrencies. The most popular are Bitcoins and Ethereums because they move predictably and are easy to trade due to their technical indicators.

However, many smaller Altcoins have higher upside potential that make them attractive to investors and traders. Some of these Altcoins have shown more than 1,000% growth.

You can use comparison tools like Coinmarketcap to know the features and benefits of coins and tokens. Cryptocompare is another site to find information like trade volume, supply, market cap, and more.

To be more updated about the current happenings in the crypto sphere, follow blogs and publications like News Bitcoin, Coindesk, and Hackernoon. You can also dig in on various social media, Quora threads, Discord channels, and other crypt0-related fora for more in-depth knowledge.

Step 6: **Mitigate risks and enhance gains by using technology**

Take advantage of the available tools and apps that help to reduce the risks and volatility of your trading portfolio. Look for an automated index that analyzes the algorithms of cryptocurrencies. One good example is the CIX100 or Cryptoindex 100.

For tracking coins to help you enhance productivity, use Delta, Blockfolio, and other special apps that provide real-time exchange prices and other valuable insights.

Two approaches used in cryptocurrency trading

There are two key techniques in trading, which have been used by traditional and crypto traders for generations. They are the Technical Analysis (TA) and Fundamental Analysis (FA).

- **Technical Analysis**

    Technical analysis is a trading technique that predicts the future price movement of the assets.

This methodology uses technical indicators like chart patterns, candlesticks, moving averages, trend lines, and more to get results.

The idea behind this analysis is that all price movements follow their own patterns and by using verifiable data, you can identify trading opportunities as well as potential entry points. This strategy works well with day trading, scalping, and even long-term investments.

- **Fundamental Analysis**

  FA or fundamental analysis is used in cryptocurrency to determine the outside forces that influence the value of the coins. It involves the evaluation of on-chain metrics and off-chain metrics to know if the digital asset is undervalued or overvalued. By analyzing the current valuation, you can decide whether to trade or not.

  On-chain metrics include the following:

    o Coin/token issuance rate (deflation/inflation)
    o Wallet addresses (dormant/active)
    o Network hash rate

- o Network applications
- o Network fees
- o Transactions

Off-line metrics are:

- o Exchange listings
- o Community engagements
- o Government regulations

Most cryptocurrency networks are public, so it is easy to access the on-chain metrics. Ethereum and Bitcoin's metrics can be tracked down using Bitinfocharts.com. This site provides a lot of useful data and is easy to navigate.

Which is better? I believe that it depends on your profile as a trader and your financial goals. If you are a swing trader or like to research and make an informed bet, fundamental analysis is for you.

If you are a day trader or someone who prefers short-term positioning multiple times in a single day, you need the technical analysis.

And as always, a smart combination of these two trading strategies can give you more positive outcomes.

Applying them both lets you identify the most favorable trading opportunities in the market because these techniques have complementary elements that will give you an edge over the competition.

Did you know that?

The Bitcoin network is very powerful and can surpass the capabilities of 500 super computers.

Important things to remember before stepping into crypto trading

- **Learn what's growing**

  Find out the top coins in terms of ease of use and tradability. The top three are of course Bitcoin, Litecoin, and Ethereum, but always keep your eyes on other growing cryptocurrencies like Zcash, Monero, Ripple, and more.

- ## Understanding order types

  If you will be trading on other exchanges that are not Coinbase.com or Cash App, you need to remember how a market order differs from a limit order and how the concept of stops works to your advantage. Cryptocurrency markets do not have strong liquidity, which is why you should be careful when placing huge market orders.

- ## Understanding blockchain

  At least learn the basics that can help you speculate price movements in the market as a response to the crypto announcements and news.

- ## Minimizing slippage

  Slippage refers to the situation where you will receive a different execution price that is different from what is intended. It results in paying an amount that is more than or less than the price you know you will be paying. It happens between the time when the order is requested and the time of exchange or the time when your order is confirmed.

It happens in fast-moving and highly volatile markets when the orders in the market could not match the traders' preferred prices due to unexpected trends and quick turns. To avoid slippage trading, traders should use a limit order rather than a market order. The limit order fulfills your order at the price you set or better.

• **Keeping your crypto account secure**

In the world of crypto, loss of access to your digital storage (wallet) or when your exchange account is hacked means saying goodbye to your coins forever. Recovering your account is a difficult process and sometimes, impossible after the hacking. I suggest you have a very strong password, 2-factor authentication, and using a hardware wallet. Always have a backup and write your pin/password/seed phrase. It is also best to encrypt them both.

- **Best to avoid margin trading if you are new in crypto trading**

  Margin trading is the practice where traders can borrow funds against their existing funds or leverage their cryptocurrency to enhance their trading power. Newcomers like you should stick first to purchasing major coins that offer good liquidity. Do not be tempted to engage in market trading until you have mastered the tricks of crypto trading.

- **Mitigate risks**

  The volatile nature of the cryptocurrency market is part of its attractiveness to investors and traders. This element can make traders win a fortune or lose a lot in an instant. Consider mitigating trading risks by applying technical analysis indicators to analyze market trends and charts. Learn and master trend trading and support and resistance techniques.

  One of the secrets of professional traders is trading Bitcoin and Ethereum (in terms of market cap) or Grayscale Bitcoin Trust (GBTC). The risk element of losing is slim or nearly impossible when you use any of these digital instruments. In essence, crypto coins with lower volumes and market caps offer a greater reward but also greater risks that can wipe out your fund.

- **Remember that derivatives have unique rule sets**

Derivatives are financial contracts that get their values from underlying assets. In cryptocurrency, it works as a proxy tool that loves speculating on the coins' future success. Holding them too long can cost you a lot of money in fees, so learn how to maximize gains by finding the best derivative in the market.

- **Don't forget that crypto trading is taxable**

Cryptocurrency is considered a capital asset or property in the U.S. It is subject to capital gains tax (long-term and short-term) when used for buying services/goods and for investment/trading purposes. Know the implications of tax in crypto trading so you will know to make the most of your trading activities.

Crypto trading is exciting and full of promises. In the beginning, it can be a bit confusing with all the technical terms and jargon but eventually, you will learn the ropes.

While the principles of trading are a bit similar to the trading stocks in the market, the execution is different.

To enjoy cryptocurrency trading and maximize its benefits, you need to do a thorough research about the assets and the market, the best crypto exchange, the most secure crypto wallet, and your chosen crypto.

Fun Trivia

Cryptokitties was the first game built with the help of Ethereum technology.
The network experienced 10% purchase increase in just one week after its launching.

FAQs

Is crypto trading profitable?

Yes, if you do it right. Like any type of trading, trading cryptocurrency requires a plan, strategies, and risk management measures. You will be in your most advantageous position if you follow your game plan and strategies

How risky is crypto trading?

Because of the high level of volatility, the risks are greater. Before you start your trading journey, assess your risk appetite first. You also need to have a game plan and risk management strategies.

Are there good cryptocurrency pairs for beginners?

No. Each cryptocurrency is different from the other, offering a range of advantages and risks to both beginners and seasoned traders. To understand them better, study each type and match it to your trading goals and strategies.

What is the best crypto trading strategy for newbies?

All strategies are good. But you should choose according to your goals. If you like long-term gains, go for position trading or HODL (holding your coins over a long period). For short-term outcomes, try day trading or scalping.

What is leverage in crypto trading?

Leverage is an approach to gain wider exposure to underlying digital assets by only paying a margin or a minimal deposit. In essence, you only pay a fraction of the entire value of the trade.

Chapter 3

What About the Crypto Market?

The cryptocurrency market is where investors and traders buy or sell Bitcoin and altcoins at current prices. It is a type of financial market where the exchange of assets happens.

The market of crypto is still relatively young but is growing very fast despite a lot of speculations and uncertainties due to the volatility factor of digital currency.

And while there are unique factors that affect the crypto market prices, global and regional economic events like inflation, political unrest, disease outbreaks, and more can influence the price

At a glance

✓ **Classifications of crypto markets**
✓ **Understanding crypto exchanges: Centralized and Decentralized**
✓ **Key factors that influence the crypto market prices**
✓ **Market trends**
✓ **Bull market versus bear market**
✓ **Ways to take advantage of the crypto bull market**
✓ **Ways to profit in a bear market**
✓ **The psychology of market cycles**
✓ **What is market sentiment analysis?**
✓ **Indicators of market sentiment**
✓ **Frequently Asked Questions (FAQs)**

Classification of crypto markets

Crypto markets can be classified into two:

- ## Spot market

   Crypto assets are bought or sold 'on the spot' in this type of market. Traders place an order, wait for the confirmation and delivery of the coins, and settle the payment right away. The context of delivery in the crypto spot market is 'immediate.' The current market price paid by the traders for the asset is called the *spot price*.

There are two types of traders in the crypto spot market. The first is the markers or trades' initiators. You are considered as a maker if you list your potential trades on your chosen exchange. An example is opening trades at your desired price points, allowing potential buyers to fulfill the orders. The second type is the takers or the traders who fulfill the orders. You are a trader if you fulfill the existing coin orders.

There is always a maker or a taker on the spot market. There are takers and markers for buy and sell orders. All the orders of traders can be viewed on the ledger or order book of the exchange. The platform has an automatic feature that matches purchase orders with existing sell orders.

- **Derivatives market**

  The derivatives are financial instruments with an underlying value that is based on the cryptocurrency's current value. They include contracts for difference (CFDs), options contracts, futures contracts, token swaps, and leveraged tokens.

  - The option contracts give traders the authority, but not an obligation, to sell or buy assets at a certain price in the future.

  - Future contracts allow crypto traders to speculate on the asset's future price. They are agreements by two parties to sell the assets on the expiry date at the last trading price. Moreover, the contract settlement is predetermined. It's either cash-settled or the underlying asset is physically delivered to the trader.

  - Leveraged tokens are tradable financial instruments. They offer leveraged exposure without the need to secure a leveraged position. Traders who prefer to use them would not be constantly worrying about funding, liquidation, margin, or collateral. These innovative products in the form of tokens derive values from perpetual futures positions.

- o Contract for difference (CFD) is a financial contract that allows traders to get the difference between the entry price and closing price. So, when the exit price is higher than the entry price, the seller of the crypto pays the buyer the difference. If the closing price is lower than the opening price, the seller gains profits.

Understanding cryptocurrency exchanges

Crypto market is commonly referred to as a cryptocurrency exchange or online platform that facilitates the trading of crypto to crypto or crypto to fiat currency/digital asset. Many crypto exchanges are trading globally and offering hundreds of available coins and tokens. They also have electronic wallets for those who engage in active trading.

Some exchanges are owned by brokers who act as an intermediary between the buyers and sellers of the cryptocurrency. Brokers earn through transaction fees and commissions.

Types of crypto exchange:

1.Centralized cryptocurrency exchange

They are operated by companies and are more reliable. Statistics reveal that about 99% of traders choose to transact business through centralized exchanges. The top exchanges based on trading volumes, traffic, and liquidity are Binance, Huobi Global, Coinbase, Kraken, and Bithumb.

Pros:

- Reliability – They have a developed and centralized platform that facilitates trading and transactions, offering more security and reliability.

- User-friendly – They work best for beginners because of their easy to navigate platform interface where traders check their accounts and balances or make transactions whenever they log in.

Cons:

- Transaction fee – Traders pay a certain amount for the services rendered and convenience. The cost of the transaction fee depends on the amounts of crypto being traded.

- Hacking risk – Centralized exchanges usually hold a great number of cryptocurrencies, which makes them a lucrative target for large-scale theft and hacking.

2. Decentralized cryptocurrency exchanges (DEX)

This type of exchange involves peer-to-peer transactions. There is no intermediary or a third party so traders do not pay transaction fees. The top DEXs are Uniswap (V2), Tokenlon, io, Blocknet, and AirSwap.

Pros:

- Anonymity – Traders are not required to provide personal information, which keeps the transactions between the seller and buyer anonymous and private.

- No hacking risk – There is no transfer of assets via a third party, so the risk of being hacked is zero.

- No market manipulation – Due to the nature of transactions, there is no market manipulation. This protects traders from wash trading and fake trading.

Cons:

- No fiat payment – Decentralized exchanges require traders to pay crypto for another crypto. This is inconvenient for beginners who want to pay fiat currency.

- Complexity – Traders who use this kind of exchange should familiarize themselves with the trading process and the platform. It is also important to memorize the password or keys to their digital wallets and have a backup to prevent losing their coins forever.

- Lack of liquidity – Since most crypto transactions are done in centralized exchanges, the decentralized exchanges experience low trading volumes that lead to a lack of liquidity. When trading volume is low, there are not enough buyers or sellers of the cryptocurrency.

Key factors that influence the crypto market prices

There is a market when demand meets supply or vice-versa. The market prices rely heavily on demand and supply. They are also highly sensitive to speculations and potential moves of buyers. In essence, the assets' prices are decided by the sellers and buyers. They hold their value because traders and investors say they do.

- **Supply and demand**

  As a unit of exchange, the bottom line of cryptocurrency is trading. The price soars when more people set their intention to buy a cryptocurrency and more sellers are willing to sell.

On the other hand, the price goes down when there are more sellers but buyers are not willing to purchase.

- **Market capitalization**
  It is the value of all circulating or existing crypto coins and how traders/investors perceive their growth rate.

- **Integration**
  It displays the easy integration of cryptocurrency into the e-commerce payment system and other existing infrastructure.

- **Endorsements**

  When notable personalities, economic experts, or celebrities positively endorse certain crypto, it can cause a hike in prices as investors and traders begin to accumulate them to ride with the tide. But remember that there is a thing called disguised advertisements.

  They are endorsements used to generate a temporary demand but leave the investors with coins that only promise immediate returns.

- **Press/Media**

  It refers to the way cryptocurrencies are portrayed in media channels and the amount of coverage they get. News stories or rumors about the potential ban of crypto or central bank control can cause price movements.

- **Key events**

  It includes major events like economic setbacks, security breaches, attacks on exchanges that reveal security flaws, and regulatory updates.

- **Disagreements in cryptocurrency communities**

  This pertains to issues over upgrades like when a certain cryptocurrency goes through a hard fork.

Market trends

Market trends refer to the perceived direction of movement of any kind of financial market within a certain period. They are identified in technical analysis with the help of trend lines, price action, or key moving averages. One peculiar characteristic of market trends is that traders believe that they have accurately determined or predicted the future event in hindsight. However, hindsight bias can produce a key impact on identifying market trends as well as making trading decisions.

The primary market trends are the bull and bear markets. The bull market symbolizes the increasing trend in the financial market or sustained uptrend, while the bear market means a declining market or sustained downtrend.

Each market trend can last from 1-3 years. It is important to remember that market trends do not entirely mean that the price is going in the given direction. A prolonged bear market has some smaller bear trends within the period and vice versa.

Both bull market and bear market offer huge opportunities for traders to gain more profits. The key is to use strong strategies to generate earnings under different market conditions. Moreover, you need to be consistent, focused, disciplined, and take advantage of greed and fear emotions.

Bull market

A bull market pertains to financial market conditions where the prices are soaring continuously or have the potential to rise soon. Whenever the demand outweighs the laws of demand and supply over an extended period, bull markets manifest. Investors and traders during bull markets are optimistic and confident as the prices continue to increase faster than the usual average rate.

Most often, bull markets occur during robust economic growth or when people become more interested in the stock markets because of higher returns on investment. Bull markets can also create 'bubbles' or when the price of the underlying asset is greater than its actual value.

Indicators of the bull market include:

- Prices rise at least 80% over an extended period
- Market indexes soar at least 15%
- Stock prices rise by 20% after the two occurrences of declines of 20%

Bull markets show four phases.

1. The first phase begins with low prices, pessimistic views about the prices, and low sentiment.

2. The second phase displays an increasing amount of trading activities and above-average economic indicators. During this period, corporate earnings and stock prices are beginning to increase. Likewise, investors and traders show more optimism.

3. The third phase shows more trading activities. The securities and market indexes reach trading highs while the dividend yields reach their lows.

4. The fourth or final phase is when there are excessive trading activities, IPO activities, and speculations. Investors and

traders are raking in profits as the earnings ratios and stock prices reach their historic highs, resulting in unraveling the bull market. During this phase, investors are also busy reacting to various negative indicators.

Did you know that?

The 3 biggest bull markets in the U.S. happened in 1860-72 during the start of the railroad industry, 1920-28 when the 19th Amendment was ratified and automobiles were invented, and 1982-99 during the launching of the Internet.

Bear market

A bear market manifests when there is a 20% or more decrease in the market index for two months. Bear markets' average length is 367 days. Bear markets happen when there is a prolonged decrease in prices. It typically occurs when there are significant factors that change the optimistic cycle of the economy.

When optimism and trust decrease, there is also a decrease in demand for the underlying asset. It creates a tipping point where the cycle hits the bottom before going up again.

The four phases of bear markets:

1. During the first phase, there is a high investor sentiment and high market prices. Eventually, they begin to take in their profits and stop trading.

2. Stock prices, corporate profits, and trading activities start to decline sharply. The economic indicators become below average and the optimistic sentiment of investors turns into panic. It is often referred to as the capitulation stage.

3. The third phase is when speculators are beginning to enter the market again, causing an increase in trading volume and market prices.

4. In this final or fourth phase, the stock prices are beginning to drop gradually. Optimism and low prices start attracting traders and investors again. This last cycle of the bear market leads to a bull market.

Ways to take advantage of crypto bull markets

The best time to buy cryptocurrency in a bull market is during the infancy or first phase period. In this way, you can sell it when the market prices reach their peak position. While there is no accurate way to determine when it will happen, your loss will be minimal.

Here are some strategies that investors and traders use during bull markets:

- **Buy and hold approach**

  It works by buying an asset, holding it for a certain period, and selling it when the market is favorable. The buy and hold approach is fueled by the bull market's optimistic condition.

- **Increase buy and hold approach**

  It is a variation of the buy and hold strategy, but involves continuous buying

of assets or security as long as the price
is rising favorably.

- **Full swing approach**

  This aggressive approach is meant to
  capitalize on the favorable conditions of
  the bull market like using the short-selling
  method to maximize profits before
  another shift happens. Short selling
  means selling borrowed assets and then
  purchasing them at lower prices.

- **Retracement addition approach**

  It refers to the brief period of price
  reversal. This is typical in the bull market,
  even if the market trend is going upward.
  Many investors and traders use this
  period within the bull market to buy more
  assets. The presumption is that the price
  of the asset will move back fast, albeit
  retroactively, and give them a discounted
  buying price.

Ways to profit in crypto bear markets

Despite the sluggishness and pessimism in bear markets, you can still make a profit. As long as there is a movement in the cryptocurrency market, the promise of profits is always possible.

Although nobody can predict when the bear markets will end or hit the bottom, you can always make a position to benefit from any favorable price movement.

Do not let your emotions of fear and doubt get into your rational thinking. Use the bear market trend to study and analyze your preferred trades. It's easy to be crippled by fear when the cryptocurrencies seem to be dipping, but their volatility can cause them to bounce so much stronger. Bitcoin has proven it so many times and other new digital assets are also showing their capability to rebound fast.

- **Buy a dip**

    Be brave and buy the dip. By setting entries beforehand, you are making a shot to lock in your position and sell your cryptocurrencies when their prices regain their strength in the market. To ensure that the opportunity to gain profit during the short period of recovery of the bear market, you should set a Full trade. It is typical for the returns to happen overnight, so by setting your entries, stop-losses, take-profits, and other safety nets, you have your gains while sleeping.

You can also automate your trades and set take-profit orders in advance so when the market takes a turn positively, you gain the most.

- **Brush up your skills on Technical Analysis**

Now is the time to have an in-depth understanding of technical analysis and how it can help you during margin or futures trading. Begin with the basics like RSI, moving averages, Fibonacci, and so on. Keep learning the indicators and soon, you will be a pro when it comes to entries and exits.

- **Learn margin trading**

Margin trading is the practice of trading using borrowed funds from brokers. The collateral of the loan is your financial asset. While it is risky, this type of trading amplifies your purchasing power. It confers tremendous potential of huge profits, but also losses. It is just an option for bold and brave traders with higher risk tolerance.

- **Dig hidden potentials**

While you can buy assets cheaply, their inherent and potential value remains. In the bear market, you don't have to rush into trading your coins because of low prices and low volumes. So, while waiting for positive price movements, research undervalued currencies that have the potential to grow big when the crypto market gets its rebound. A coin that has dropped more than 70% may look less valuable when it lost its all-time high but can rebound with a bang. Sometimes, the reason why assets fall is due to its still developing platform or loss of interest of the crowd.

- **Scalp and earn**

Scalping is an attempt to earn money from small price movements in the market. A scalp trader can position himself many times within short periods to maximize the opportunities of market inefficiency and price movement. This kind of trading strategy necessitates performing a very quick technical analysis.

- **Educate yourself**

In the bear market, there is no rush to keep refreshing your assets portfolio or do frenzy trading to maximize gains. It is time to upgrade your skills and knowledge like researching the next set of phenomenal coins, understanding leverages, or learning how to identify the vital signs of market reversal. All your learnings during the bear market will increase your chances when the bull market starts to manifest.

The Psychology of Market Cycles

All financial markets have cyclical nature or have an expansion and contraction cycle. **Market cycles** are trends or patterns that manifest at different periods. They usually emerge when a certain asset class outperforms the other classes. Within the same market cycle, some asset classes underperform because of varying market conditions.

Market cycles happen because of the **market sentiment** or the collective attitude of investors and traders towards the asset. It is true to all financial markets, which include the crypto market. The overall moods, thoughts, and feelings of participants can move the prices of the cryptocurrency, creating a psychological market cycle.

The idea that the price shifts in the market reflect the emotions of the traders is called **market psychology**. It is an important topic in behavioral economics because of its impact on economic decisions. A positive market sentiment creates a bullish trend (bull market) with prices of crypto increasing continuously. The opposite trend results in a bear market, with prices declining continuously.

Uptrend

When there is positive market sentiment, the demand for the assets increases, and the supply decreases. When it happens, there is an overall strong attitude, belief, optimism, and greed in the market climate. These emotions contribute to a very strong buying activity.

And it does not stop there. It is common in the market cycles during an uptrend to see a retroactive effect. It means that as the crypto prices soar, the market sentiment becomes more positive and drives the prices higher.

During this period, there is a prevailing sense of greed that generates a financial bubble. This drives a lot of traders and investors to accumulate more assets, believing that the positive trend will continue. They tend to be irrational and lose sight of the asset's actual value. More assets are sold during this *distribution stage*, creating a sideways market movement.

Downtrend

In contrast, a downtrend brings a negative market sentiment that lessens the demand and increases the supply of assets.

The investors and traders become complacent after losing the euphoric feelings once the market takes a negative turn. And when the prices of cryptocurrencies continue to decline, the sentiment of the participants turns into anxiety, denial, and panic.

As the prices drop, crypto investors and traders start questioning why it is happening. This gives rise to anxiety and unacceptance or denial of the fact that there is a downtrend. Many of them continue to hold on to their positions because they believe that the positive market trend will resume soon. Others feel that it is too late for them to sell their assets.

Panic comes in as the cryptocurrency prices dip down tremendously. At this juncture, the prevailing emotion is fear. Almost everyone wants to sell their digital assets. This is the period of market capitulation or when crypto owners sell their coins at a losing price.

The downtrend period halts when the crypto volatility decreases. This leads to the eventual stabilization of the market. There will be sideways movements that contribute to the renewed feelings of optimism and hope. This period is called the *accumulation stage*.

What is market sentiment analysis?

While market sentiment does not reflect the crypto fundamentals, it can impact its price. This is why traders are constantly reviewing the current sentiment of the majority of participants. A **market sentiment analysis** can be used to predict price movements. It entails tracking the dynamics of the market and the overall attitudes of the participants to fully understand their fear or hype emotion about a certain asset. Aside from providing vital insights on the market demand, analyzing the market sentiment can potentially predict favorable trends that will give you profits.

Like the fundamental analysis or technical analysis, analyzing the market helps traders make sound decisions. Combining the pertinent data from the three methods is a great idea.

- It helps you have a clear concept of short and mid-term price action.

- It helps you discover profitable trading opportunities.

- It helps you get hold of your emotional state.

To perform a market sentiment analysis, you need the opinions, ideas, and views of the participants. You can start by checking the relevant crypto channels and social media platforms. Twitter is one of the most popular social channels among crypto fans.

Joining official crypto forums, Telegram groups, and Discord servers will also help you in analyzing the market sentiment. But be mindful of scammers lurking in these pages or communities. They are always ready to prowl on easy prey, so make sure that you are doing your own analysis and not swayed by some 'sweet talks' of some traders who establish themselves as 'experts'.

You may also consider the following methods:

- Keeping yourself up to date by following crypto blogs and media portals that publish the latest news and trends. Check out Binance News, CoinDesk, Binance Blogs, and Bitcoin Magazine.

- Tracking social mentions with the help of data collection software tools.

- Checking the pricing signals and indicators of market sentiment on CoinMarketCap. They are collated from various reliable sources and the summaries are the current market sentiment.

- Setting alerts or tracking huge transactions by 'whales' or individuals/organizations that are holding a great number of certain cryptocurrencies. They have enough crypto coins or tokens and can create a ripple on the prices by selling or buying large amounts.

- Measuring the hype level that surrounds cryptocurrency with the help of Google Trends.

Indicators of market sentiment

Market sentiment indicators represent the underlying emotions that can change a bull market into a bear market or vice versa. Using a scale or graphic tools, you get to view the current sentiment of the participants.

One of the widely-used tools is the Bitcoin Crypto Fear & Greed Index. It displays the market greed or fear using the scale of 0-100. It uses 5 information sources to get an accurate result.

They are the crypto volatility, dominance, trends, market volume, and social media.

Another useful tool is Augmento's Bull & Bear Index. This market sentiment indicator uses social media impressions through its artificial intelligence (AI) software. It can analyze 93 topics and sentiments by tapping the conversations on Bitcointalk, Twitter, and Reddit.

FAQs

Why are financial markets important?

Financial markets play a great role in economic activities like growth opportunities, investment, commerce & trade. The fundamental functions of any type of financial market are to provide a free market for an efficient flow of capital and allow investors to earn capital gains.

Who are the key players in financial markets?

Investors who want efficient capital and asset allocation. Speculators who view asset classes like cryptocurrency and make directional bets on their future values.

The brokers are intermediaries that bring sellers and buyers of assets together.

The arbitrageurs who are on the lookout for anomalies or mispricing would always find a way to gain from them.

The hedgers who use the derivative markets in mitigating different types of risks.

Chapter 4

Prepping Up for Trading

Cryptocurrency trading has elements of volatility and unpredictability, hence the importance of making a trading plan that will guide you in making smart decisions. You also need an effective trading strategy or combination of strategies to achieve your goals. Having a smart plan and putting your chosen trading strategies in action helps you when to cut losses, when to take profits, which market to trade, or where to find other growth opportunities.

At a glance

- ✓ **What is a trading plan?**
- ✓ **Do you need a trading plan?**
- ✓ **How to create a solid and winning trading plan?**
- ✓ **Frequently Asked Questions**

What is a trading plan?

A trading plan is your comprehensive trading tool. It is a personal plan that will guide you when, how much, and what to trade. It is your roadmap to successful cryptocurrency trading or any type of trading you want to try.

This plan is a written document that is well-researched and systematic. It can be customized according to your goals, expectations, strategies, and other parameters. It outlines the ways to find opportunities and execute trades, what securities to trade, how large the position you will take, how to manage the positions, and the rules when or when not to trade.

A trading plan may include the following:

- Your motivation or reason for trading cryptocurrency
- Your goals and financial objectives
- Your time commitment
- Your risk tolerance or level of attitude to risks
- Your personal risk management rules
- Your available capital
- Your strategies

- Your chosen trading markets
- Your record-keeping method (trading journal)

Do you need a trading plan?

The answer is a resounding "YES!"

Your trading plan clearly defines your trading parameters, helping you make logical decisions like when to trade or when to stop your losses. During heated moments in the trading market, like when a bullish trend is happening, your trading plan helps you avoid acting irrationally.

Other benefits of having a trading plan are:

- It makes trading easier – You have done all the planning and researching beforehand, so all you need to do is to trade your crypto according to your trading parameters.

- It promotes better discipline – Trading is full of growth opportunities, but not all good prospects can give you the edge you desire and may lead to disastrous events like losing all your crypto in one move. A trading plan helps you stick to your goals and observe your pre-set limitations.

- It helps in making more objective choices and decisions- Because you already know when to cut trading losses or when you should take your profits, you do not let strong emotions obscure your logical reasoning.

- It provides room for improvement – By reviewing your trading journal, you learn the lessons from your previous trading mistakes. It helps you make better judgments and moves.

How to create a solid and winning trading plan?

Remember the famous cliché, 'failing to plan is planning to fail'? It may sound a little glib, but it works excellently in the business sphere, especially in crypto trading. A winning trading plan is what separates successful traders from average traders. They also methodologically follow their sound and strategic plan.

Every trading plan is unique to traders. While you can copy or use the techniques of other traders, you need to consider the factors that reflect your choices and trading styles.

Here are the vital steps you need to do to build your perfect master plan:

Step 1: Outline your trading motivation

Why do you want to join the trading world? Generally, people would say it's all about the lucrative profits. But it is important to write down your reasons why you want to trade.

Step 2: Define your trading goals.

Do not just write a simple statement like "I want to gain profits." You should write SMART (specific, measurable, attainable, relevant, and time-bound) goals. A good example is "This year, I want to add value to my financial portfolio by up to 25%." You can break down your big goal into mini-goals in a week, month, or year. Review your goals and their progress regularly.

Step 3: Know your trading style.

You should know your trading style based on your attitude to risk, your personality, and the amount of time you can commit to trading. Trading requires time if you want to gain a lot of profits.

It is important to set a specific period to do your trading activities. It also depends on the kind of trading style method you will use.

A quick review of the 4 primary trading styles:

- Day trading – It involves opening and closing several trades during the same day. You will be spending hours in front of your computer or mobile screen if it is your choice.

- Position trading – It is about holding your positions for several weeks, months, or years. It does not require too much of your time, knowing it is a long-term trading strategy.

- Scalping – This entails making several trades every day, for a few minutes or seconds, to make small profits that eventually will add up to a huge amount of money.

- Swing trading – It is about holding your trading positions over a few days or weeks and taking advantage of the price movements in the medium-term market.

Step 4: Set your risk-reward ratio.

In trading, you may lose many times, but you can still earn consistent profits. The key is setting your risk-reward ratio. How much are you willing to risk in your every trade? Setting your risk level is important. It should vary from 1% to 5% of your entire portfolio.

Knowing your limit will help you get out of the trade without losing much when the market does not favor your position. A 1:3 risk-reward ratio or higher is ideal.

For example, you risk $100 on a trade with a $300 potential gain. This shows that your target profit is double the rate of your potential loss.

Step 5: Decide the amount of your trading capital.

Your capital should be the amount of money you are willing to lose in the worst trading scenarios. It is extremely important to avoid risking more than you can afford or your egg nest just for the thrill of trading to have more. There are plenty of risks in trading, so you need to do your math before you start your game plan.

	Trivia *Backtesting is a practice that allows traders to test an idea with the help of historical data and its viability.*

FAQs

What are the crucial questions that my trading plan should answer?

- What are your primary reasons why you want to become a trader?
- What do you want to achieve from crypto trading?
- What are your biggest strengths and weaknesses?
- What are your plans to leverage your strengths and address the weaknesses?
- Do you have plans that will set you apart from the majority of crypto traders who failed in the past?
- What market/markets do you plan to trade your crypto in and why?

- What trading systems are you going to use when entering or exiting trades?

- What are the trading equipment and software you are going to use in trading?
- Do you have a plan to withdraw your profit or reinvest it?

Does a trading plan guarantee my success in altcoin trading?

There is no guarantee of success, but it eliminates major roadblocks and helps you hone your skills. A solid trading plan is about avoiding failure.

Can I change my trading plan?

A trading plan is not static and can evolve based on your skills or changing market conditions.

Chapter 5

The Cryptocurrency that Started It All: Bitcoin

Bitcoin (denoted "฿") is often called the currency of the internet. It is abbreviated as XBT or BTC. It is both a technology and virtual currency that works like digital cash for the exchange of goods or services. Bitcoin is accessible to all, regardless of gender, religion, ethnicity, or political beliefs.

In the context of value, it is the undisputed king of cryptocurrency due to the stability of its network. This electronic cash system has proved its worth amidst the ups and downs of the financial market. Until today, it kept its independent nature without the intervention of any central authority.

The versatile nature of Bitcoin has caught the interest of private corporations and individuals who are on the lookout for lucrative ways to multiply their wealth and passive income.

As a frontrunner, Bitcoin inspired the subsequent explosion of new players in the cryptocurrency, creating a legion of spinoffs and users.

In terms of popularity, user base, and market capitalization, Bitcoin is the leader of the crypto pack. It has become not just the trendsetter but the cryptocurrencies' de-facto standard. It comprises half of the crypto market and sustains its claim as the most-sought instrument in crypto trading. Its history depicts a series of exponential growth and profitability, making a lot of investors and traders multimillionaires in just a few years of owning Bitcoin.

At a glance
- ✓ **A glimpse in Bitcoin's history**
- ✓ **Growing pains**
- ✓ **The value of Bitcoin**
- ✓ **Classification of Bitcoin**
- ✓ **Bitcoin transactions**
- ✓ **Reasons to trade Bitcoin**
- ✓ **Risks that you should be aware of**
- ✓ **Are you ready to trade Bitcoin?**
- ✓ **Best Bitcoin trading strategies**
- ✓ **Popular trading styles for advanced traders**
- ✓ **Frequently Asked Questions (FAQs**

Bitcoin's history

Bitcoin is the first successful feat after so many attempts to create digital currencies using cryptography, which is the science of generating and breaking codes. It was a brainchild of Satoshi Nakamoto, whose real identity until now is still a big mystery. Along with Bitcoin, he also developed the blockchain database.

On January 3, the 'genesis block' or Block O was mined. It is the first-ever mined block of Bitcoin. Nakamoto introduced the first bitcoin software version to the public on January 8, 2009, via the Cryptography Mailing List. And on January 9, 2009, the official mining of Bitcoin commenced with Block 1.

The first-ever Bitcoin transaction in the real world happened on May 22, 2010, when programmer Laszlo Hanyecz bought two Papa John's pizzas worth 10,000 BTC in Jacksonville, Florida. Fast forward today, the said amount is worth over $600 million.

Growing Pains

The journey to the top is not easy for this revolutionary currency. It needed to carve a path on its own.

As expected, many were doubtful about its longevity and success. Not a lot of investors and traders would gamble their money for a new player in the industry, especially because cryptocurrency was still new and has not proven its stability and credibility in the financial market.

Since its inception, Bitcoin has displayed significant ups and downs, violent crashes, and uptrend growth. Its recent all-time high happened in March 2021, when one Bitcoin reached an all-time high of $61,683. Way back then during its creation, 1 BTC was worth $0.008.

What's the difference?

Bitcoin (with capital B) refers to this crypto as an entity, while bitcoin (small letter b) refers to the quantity or the units.

The Value of Bitcoin

Bitcoin is not a coin, but a file with certain values that can be used for initiating payments to goods or services. It is a digital software with a unique set of protocols, rules, and processes that exists in the virtual cloud.

Bitcoin's real value comes from its code, infrastructure, scarcity, and adoption. It has no intrinsic value or is backed by gold and silver. Intrinsic value refers to any kind of currency that has the backing of the government, precious metals, or the people's trust over the government.

Bitcoin and Altcoins do not have these elements, but they have the trust of millions of people. The participants in the crypto network are the miners and traders who trust Bitcoin decides its price based on supply and demand.

In addition, like traditional currencies, Bitcoin has value because it is accepted as a unit of exchange and as a store of value. It also possesses the 6 major attributes of successful currencies:

- Scarcity – Bitcoin's finite availability greatly increases its demand in the market. Currently, more than 18 million bitcoins are in circulation. Mining new bitcoins will stop when it reaches the 21 million limit.

- Utility – Bitcoin's blockchain technology is one of its selling points. The trustless and decentralized nature of this ledger system makes global transactions more convenient and safe.

Moreover, blockchain technology is also flexible and can be utilized beyond the crypto world.

- Divisibility – The smallest unit of Bitcoin is Satoshi, which is equal to 0.00000001 One Bitcoin is equivalent to 100,000,000 Satoshis. The lowest transaction value in Bitcoin is 546 Satoshis.

- Durability – Cryptocurrencies are not susceptible to deformity or other physical harms that will render them unusable. This characteristic makes Bitcoin tremendously valuable. It will continue its existence in the blockchain as long as there are transactions by the owners and traders.

- Transportability – Bitcoin can be transferred from one user to another in a matter of seconds, regardless of the amount of the transaction via crypto wallets and exchanges.

- Counterfeitability – Attempting to counterfeit bitcoin is incredibly difficult because of the decentralized and complex structure of its blockchain ledger system.

How do you classify Bitcoin?

Is it an asset class, a store of value, a payment system, or a kind of currency? Bitcoin can be all these, making it a versatile virtual phenomenon that is exchanged through blockchain technology or publicly distributed ledger. There is no human-to-human intervention during the transactions.

Technically, Bitcoin is simply a list. For example, Person C transferred X bitcoin to Person D, who sent bitcoin to Person E. All these transactions are processed, tallied, and recorded permanently in the blockchain. Bitcoin's blockchain is open to the public, so anyone can view past and current transactions.

This popular virtual currency is regarded by the Commodity Futures Trading Commission (CFTC) as a commodity while the Internal Revenue Service (IRS) sees it as a property and needs to be taxed.

Bitcoin transactions

The lifecycle of Bitcoin transactions begins when a user creates a request to transfer funds to another user. To authorize the spending of funds, a valid electronic signature is necessary. Then, the transaction is broadcast, confirmed, and shared by the network nodes until it reaches the minding node for full validation and recording. All transactions are irreversible and added to the system's blocks.

It involves three elements to be successful:

- **Transaction input -** It is the bitcoin address from where the fund will come from. Your bitcoin address is a string of randomly generated alphanumeric characters. Along with this address is your private key to help you access it and restrict anyone to view or steal your bitcoins.

- **Transaction output -** It is the public bitcoin address or e-wallet address where the fund goes.

- **Amount** – It is the value (number of Satoshi) of Bitcoin that you want to send to another user for whatever purpose you agreed on.

All these elements are registered in the blockchain and encrypted for security reasons. It allows users to trace all Bitcoin transactions since it was first created, without identifying the user information. People who are viewing the history on the blockchain can only see the public key next to every transaction.

Reasons to trade Bitcoin

Bitcoin is the big brother of all crypto coins that opens the great path of trading and investing in digital currency.

Its popularity is influenced by the following factors:

- 24/7 trading

    Bitcoin trading does not stop, except for regular network maintenance. Traders can open or exit their positions 24/7 in a year. The crypto exchanges are all web-based so you trade around the clock, whenever or wherever you are.

- Global appeal

  Bitcoin operates in more than 90% of countries in the world. This simply means that you can engage in trading or transfer crypto funds even if you are in another part of the continent. Moreover, it is gaining more recognition as a medium of exchange and payment options.

- High volatility

  Traders are fascinated with the uptrends of Bitcoin prices, which means that speculating the movements is exciting and can give you a sudden windfall profit. Of course, the risks are high and could lead to significant losses.

- Deregulated landscape

  The lack of regulations makes it more attractive to people who want to take their trading to the next level. While crypto trading is still not mature, the impressive performance of Bitcoin including its ups and downs gives it clout of influence that appeals to investors and traders.

Risks you should be aware of

For beginners, trading Bitcoin can be riskier. It is necessary to be aware of the obvious and hidden risks before you invest your money in bitcoins. This will help you avoid expensive mistakes that can rob your confidence in trading.

To avoid traps and pitfalls, understand the following factors:

- Dangers of volatility

  Bitcoin is regarded as the most volatile asset in the financial market, much more than gold and stocks. It's true that volatility brings greater profitability in day trading style, it is also surrounded by unpredictability and doubt elements.

- Margin trading

  Margin trading using derivatives multiples profit potential as well as the risk. In worst scenarios, traders who engage in margin trading suffer from a loss that exceeds their deposit.

- Transaction costs

  The cost of transaction fees and charges during the buying and selling of Bitcoin vary. If you are into day trading and doing multiple trades, this can be a significant risk matter. Derivatives including binary options and CFDs can help you mitigate the risk.

- Exchange risks

  Always do business with reputable and trusted exchange platforms or brokers with a good reputation in the financial market. It is important that the platform is secure and prevents glitches during transactions.

  Also, deal with people you trust to avoid kissing goodbye to your bitcoin because once you transfer it, the only person who can get it is the recipient.

- Regulation

  Many governments are looking at Bitcoin and other cryptocurrencies with so much interest, trying to figure out how to impose stringent regulations.

While it is not yet happening, some countries already ban crypto.

> **Fun Trivia**
> *Bitcoin is a global phenomenon that is constantly in trading motion.*
> *It is believed that an average bitcoin transaction is 350,000 or about 4 transactions every second.*

Are you ready to start trading Bitcoin?

To trade Bitcoin, here's a step by step beginner's guide:

Step 1: Know the price

Head over to an exchange broker or index to find out the current price of Bitcoin. Its price goes up and down because of the impact of supply, integration, bad press, or key events.

Step 2: Select how to get exposure to Bitcoin

There are 3 ways to get exposure:

- Buying through an exchange – traders who like to have direct ownership of their bitcoins and go for a buy-and-hold strategy.

- Trading bitcoin derivatives – traders speculate on the price using CFDs without the need to buy coins. It allows you to take a position by 'going short' or 'going long.'

- Crypto 10 index- a market capitalization-weighted index (B10 index) of top ten performing cryptocurrencies. Market capitalization is the result of multiplying the current market value of the crypto against the US dollar by the number of units of the given coin.

Step 3: Choose a broker

Decide which broker or exchange to use for trading Bitcoin. Some brokers allow trading the

Bitcoin's underlying assets via spread bets or CFDs.

Step 4: Set a trading capital

Start small and trade only what you can afford to lose. Again, trading is about speculations so strike while the iron is hot but proceed with caution.

Step 5: Decide on your trading strategy

The trading strategy is your preferred style of trading. It will determine what kind of trader you are. Generally, you will fall into one of these types:

- Day traders – those who take advantage of short term price movements in the crypto market

- Scalpers – active traders who make multiple traders every single day to gain small profits

- Swing traders – those who seek to capture market trends based on the results of their technical analysis

- Passive traders – people who hold their positions to gain long term profits

Step 6: Set stops and limits

They are important tools to manage the risks in trading. A **stop order** allows traders to set the price point where your order will be executed. It works to limit your losses, protect profits, as well as initiate new trading positions.

A **limit order** lets traders set the minimum price that will trigger execution. There is an advanced setting that allows you to choose **Post Only** or **Allow Taker**. Enabling Post Only keeps the limit order on the order book. When it is filled, you will be charged a **Maker Fee**.

Allow Taker allows the market order's fulfillment whenever it crosses the spread, regardless if it is only a portion of the total order. The **Taker Fees** are calculated based on the portion.

Step 7:   Open and monitor your trade

Opening a trade means buying when you believe that the price of the Bitcoin will rise or selling your coin when you think that the price will fall. Monitoring the market is necessary to ensure that the Bitcoin price is moving favorably.

Step 8:   Close your position

Whenever you feel uncomfortable, cut your loss by closing your position. You can also close it if you like to take your profit. All losses are deducted from your trading account balance and the profits are trading directly to your account.

Do you know that?

El Salvador was the first country that recognized Bitcoin as legal tender.
It happened on June 9, 2021.

What are the best bitcoin trading strategies?

Trading bitcoin for profit is considered the universal strategy in cryptocurrency trading. Bitcoin is accepted as a trading and payment instrument. It is still the hottest trading instrument in the cryptocurrency market, much more than gold trading, oil trading, or stock trading.

Investors and traders believe in bitcoin's ability due to its revolutionary blockchain technology. In essence, the best BTC trading style is the one that aligns with your goals, capital, and risk appetite. Moreover, the strategy should be 85% price action and 15% strategy that utilizes indicators.

Strategies are necessary because they serve as your guide in trading and mitigate huge losses. Without a clear and solid strategy, you will be blindsided by a lot of distracting factors in the trading sphere.

A trading strategy helps you maximize your capital by knowing when to take a position and when to get your profit before the market turns around.

An effective Bitcoin strategy should include the tools and indicators you will use, the setup to take, the factors that will trigger your entries and exits, the elements that can influence the sizing of your positions, and the ways you measure and record the performance of your portfolio.

To find out the right one for you, here's a list of the recommended strategies for beginners:

- Trend trading

   Several times in its decade-long history, Bitcoin has proven itself as a powerful trend driver. Trend traders do not want to experience FOMO (fear of missing out), so they keep themselves updated for any significant events or news that can influence the Bitcoin price.

Trend trading involves holding your position open in hours, days, or even months. This is because you believe that the ongoing trend will continue moving to its current direction or create another trend. Traders who use this strategy predict the potential direction of the market price's momentum through technical analysis.

The most effective momentum and trend indicators are the stochastic oscillators, moving averages, and RSI (relative strength index).

- Swing trading

It is another trading style that suits beginners because of its elements of taking a long time to play out, allowing traders to think about their decisions and choices. It necessitates observing the 'natural swing' of the bitcoin price cycles and positioning until the desired profit is achieved or holding out until the price movement stops. It may involve holding the position open for more than 24 hours but less than a month.

In essence, swing trading is a crossover of day trading and trend trading.

- ## HODLing

HODLing (holding on for dear life) is a popular bitcoin trading strategy that was coined in 2013. It was the year when the price of bitcoins was radically falling and one of the users typed 'hodling' instead of 'holding' to show his intention to sustain his position.

The term eventually evolved and has become a trading strategy that involves sticking around in a long position in the belief that the price will soon peak. However, this strategy is risky. You need to have a solid risk management plan for this option.

- ## Hedging

Hedging bitcoin involves opening several strategic trades to avoid or lessen the risk to current positions. It is a strategy used by bitcoin traders who believe that the price will experience a short-term decline at the soonest time.

To prevent huge losses, you need to open a short bitcoin position, which means selling your digital assets based on the current price in the market. If the dreaded scenario happens, you can easily buy your bitcoin for a lower cost and earn profit from the price difference. Another way to hedge bitcoins is by using CFDs (contracts for difference).

This derivative product lets you trade without the need to buy the underlying asset. You just need to buy a portion of the entire asset to leverage your trading exposure.

Popular trading styles for advanced bitcoin traders:

- Day trading

    This is for active and savvy traders who enjoy action every single day. You can day trade from any location 24/7 for 365 days. You can go short or long, be bearish or bullish because every day offers new profit and growth opportunities.

    This volatile market can display price swings in just a matter of hours. Multiple trading opportunities can happen within 24 hours.

Because of its volatility and liquidity, there will always be a high number of growth potential and profitable windows. Also, bitcoin allows low overhead for big trades. To maximize the benefits of day trading, pay attention to the developing trends in the market and technical indicators which include moving averages, relative strength, volume, and oscillators.

OBV or On Balance Volume is one of the most effective day trading bitcoin indicators. It works by analyzing the total amount of money that flows in and out of the financial instrument. This indicator studies the price activity and volume to predict the direction of the market price.

- Breakout trading

This strategy requires traders to enter the market during the trend and be prepared for the potential 'breakout' of the bitcoin price from its previous range. The rationale of this trading style is based on the belief that when the market breaks due to resistance level or key support, there will be major volatility.

You should watch out for key points and enter the market at once if you want to ride the uptrend until it completes its cycle. In identifying the levels of support and resistance, you need to consider the technical indicators which include the RSI (relative strength index) and the MACD (moving average convergence divergence) as well as the volume level as a confirmation signal.

- Scalping

It is a type of day-trading style that focuses on short-term positioning to earn substantial profits. It requires traders to make consistent attempts repeatedly to take advantage of the small price movements of bitcoin in the market. The rationale behind this strategy is by exploiting small moves with consistency, the risks are reduced and small profits will lead to a big amount.

FAQs

How much capital do I need to start buying Bitcoin?

There is no rule about the minimum purchase but some crypto exchanges have a minimum order size that you should take into consideration. You may also end up paying higher transaction fees if you make small purchases.

What affects the price of Bitcoin?

The price of Bitcoin is generally influenced by the following:

- supply and demand of Bitcoin

- the exchanges it trades on

- the number of competing coins or altcoins

- the cost of Bitcoin mining

- the cost of incentives given to the miners of bitcoin

- the regulations that govern bitcoin's sale

- internal governance of Bitcoin (due to the absence of core authority, it relies on developers and miners to protect the blockchain network)

How can I acquire Bitcoin?

There are several ways to obtain bitcoins – buy at an exchange, receive it as payment for services or goods, exchange bitcoins with other holders, and earn through competitive crypto mining.

Is it easy to make a payment using Bitcoin?

Compared to credit or debit card purchases, using Bitcoin to pay your purchases is easier. You just need to enter the receiver's address, input the amount, and press SEND. You can also scan a QR code to complete the transaction.

What are the advantages I get from Bitcoin?

Bitcoin offers payment freedom – no bureaucracy, no geographical borders, or bank holidays. It has different levels of transfer fees and there are no fees when receiving bitcoins. Transactions are secure, anonymous, and irreversible. All transactions are neutral and transparent in the blockchain (without revealing your identity).

What are the disadvantages of using Bitcoin?

The number of merchants who accept crypto payment is still relatively small and many people are still unaware of cryptocurrency. Bitcoin's volatility is also another factor.

Is Bitcoin a fraud scheme?

No. A Ponzi scheme preys on its investors and when there are no new participants, the network collapses and affects the most recent investors. Bitcoin is a decentralized software project where all transactions utilize blockchain technology and prevent fraudulent representations about the investment.

Is Bitcoin a cult?

No. Bitcoin is a virtual asset that is accepted as a payment option as well as a trading and investment instrument. Whereas, a cult is a group of devout followers who are invested in an idea or mission. The misconception is borne out of the craze that bitcoin has caused, attracting a lot of believers.

Is Bitcoin a bubble?

Some people think that Bitcoin is a bubble because of the phenomenal 10 million % increase of its value since its conception. A bubble is expected to burst after some time. However, Bitcoin proves that while its price goes up and down due to the demand and supply factors, it is still attracting more users across the globe.

Chapter 6

The Moment to Shine for Altcoins

After the success of bitcoin, a lot of digital currencies appear in the market. They are collectively known as Altcoins or alternative coins. The term Altcoin is derived from the combination of the words 'alt' (alternative) and 'coin' (cryptocurrency) to imply that it is a type of crypto other than Bitcoin.

At a glance

- ✓ What are altcoins?
- ✓ How do they differ from Bitcoin?
- ✓ What are the pros and cons when you invest in altcoins?
- ✓ What are the different kinds of altcoins?
- ✓ Tokens: Security versus Utility
- ✓ Meet the most important altcoins
- ✓ Altcoin Watchlist: DeFi coins and tokens
- ✓ Why you should trade altcoins
- ✓ How to trade altcoins?
- ✓ Must-have altcoins to own before the AltSeason
- ✓ Altcoin trading guide for beginners
- ✓ Beginners' trading mistakes to avoid
- ✓ Frequently Asked Questions (FAQs)

What are Altcoins?

Altcoins are patterned after the best features of Bitcoin. They both use the basic framework, blockchain technology, peer-to-peer system, and code sharing functionality.

To distinguish themselves from Bitcoin and create their own market, some Altcoins use a different mechanism to validate their transactions or create blocks. Others offer additional features or breakthrough capabilities to attract users.

Slowly but surely, Altcoins are gaining traction in the financial world. In March 2021, CoinMarketCap reported that alternative coins gained more than 40% share of the crypto market.

And while they tend to follow the trajectory of Bitcoin, a lot of analysts and experts are claiming that in due time, Altcoins will be having their own trading signals.

This is because the ecosystem of crypto investing is already maturing and more markets for Altcoins are emerging.

(Circulating supply and price are subject to changes)
Source: Gold Price Org July 20,2021

Cryptocurrency	Market Cap	Circulating Supply	Current Price
Bitcoin	601,438,654, 476	18,762,718	$32,038
Ethereum	230,431,849, 444	116,784,211	$1,975. 81
Tether	62,396,028, 960	62,113,782, 909	$1
Binance Coin	45,066,256, 841	154,533,652	$292.69
Cardano	38,122,956, 586	32,066,390, 668	$1.19
XRP	26,436,361, 719	46,265,302, 471	$1
USD Coin	26,852,704, 393	26,817,435, 136	$1
Dogecoin	26,245,606, 286	130,521,667, 625	$0.20
Polkadot	12,756,321, 315	1,012,065, 607	$12.63
Binance USD	11,348,554, 555	11,300,776, 231	$1
Bitcoin	8,068,168,		

Cash	825	18,795,512	$429.66
Litecoin	7,824,010,397	66,752,415	$117.47
Chainlink	6,792,245,054	440,009,554	$15.47
Stellar	5,273,932,865	23,306,946,972	$0.23
Monero	3,539,110,083	17,957,194	$197.48

How do they differ from Bitcoin?

Every type of Altcoin has its own set of rules. In terms of mining new coins, Altcoins like Litecoin can produce new coins in a matter of 2.5 minutes. Bitcoin only mines bitcoins every 10 minutes using costly hardware. Litecoin and other alternative cryptocurrencies use new coins using common computer hardware.

Altcoins also work to improve the perceived limitations of Bitcoin, which makes them more interesting in the eyes of traders and investors. They introduced smart contracts where Bitcoin has limited capacity. Instead of using Proof-of-Work (PoW), Bitcoin's consensus mechanism to validate transactions and make blocks in the blockchain, they use the Proof-of-Stake (PoS).

What are the Pros and Cons when you invest in altcoins?

Pros

- The variety of available Altcoins offers the fulfillment of Bitcoin's promise that cryptocurrency can be a medium of everyday transactions.

- They claim to be Bitcoin's 'better versions' because they fill the gap in the crypto market.

- Traders and investors have a wide range of Altcoins that offer different functionalities.

- Low transaction fees

Cons

- Compared to Bitcoin, they have a smaller market in terms of investment

- Difficulty in distinguishing different kinds of Altcoins and their functions, making investors confused and disinterested

- The lack of defined investment criteria and regulations makes them more volatile than Bitcoin

- History of 'dead' Altcoins that left investors with huge losses

- Value volatility

- Higher potential for fraud and scams

Trivia

There are 4 buckets of altcoins – native cryptocurrencies, tokens, stablecoins, and forks.

What are the different kinds of altcoins?

Altcoins are classified according to their consensus mechanism and functionality. They include the following:

- Stablecoins

  Stablecoins are Altcoins that derive their market values from a basket of underlying assets (precious metals, fiat currencies, other cryptocurrencies). The basket represents the security that traders can redeem during the worst bad market day.

  Most Stablecoins use government-backed or fiat security. Tether (USDT) and USDC are examples of fiat-backed crypto coins. DAI is a crypto-backed Stablecoin. Commodity-backed (oil or precious metals) are the Paxos Gold and Tether Gold.

  Because of their stability, many investors tend to purchase Stablecoins while waiting for the crypto market to show favorable events. They are also great for payment purposes or money transfers anywhere in the globe.

  Stablecoins are highly tradeable and liquid. Their value does not change until you decide to move it into another altcoin or Bitcoin.

- **Mining-based**

  Mining-based altcoins are created through Proof-of-Work (PoW) method. They are mined through algorithms or solving complex problems. Litecoin, Zcash, and Monero are examples of mining-based altcoins.

  There are also pre-mined coins that are distributed before their listing in the crypto markets. XRP of Ripple is an example of this kind.

- **Security tokens**

  Security tokens are like the traditional stocks, bonds, equities, or derivatives that hold the tradable value of the external assets. These digital tokens guarantee a dividend payout, equity, or ownership. The price of security tokens appreciates over time. They are often sold to traders and investors through ICOs or initial coin offerings.

In essence, they are investment contracts that represent the users' legal ownership of a particular digital or physical asset.

Ownership rights are verified by the network within the blockchain. Once fully verified, security tokens can be traded away for another type of assets, stored in electronic wallets, or used as loan collateral.

One of the forms of security tokens is the securitized tokens. They are usually set up by startup companies and subject to compliance with the regulations of the Federal Laws. They are offered to the interested investors through Security Token Offering (STO).

Examples of security tokens are Bcap (Blockchain Capital, Sia Funds, and Science Blockchain.

- Utility tokens

  Utility tokens are utilized in exchange for services or redeem rewards. They are also called app coins or digital coupons that hold special discounts or access to the product or service.

  They are blockchain-based assets that are sold by fundraisers or companies to purchase their soon-to-be-introduced product or service.

  Utility tokens do not have intrinsic value or pay dividends. They are not considered an instrument of investment and are not subjected to Federal laws compliance.

  But utility tokens can provide holders with the right to use the network, help to build the system's internal economy, and vote for the well-being of the network.

  Examples of utility tokens are Filecoin, Civic, and Siacon.

Tokens: Security Vs Utility

Tokens are not cryptocurrency coins, but they play an important role in the success of blockchain. They are a representation of value, asset, voting rights, access rights, stake, or anything issued by companies, in particular startups. They are offered through a crowd or public sale – STO (Security Token Offerings) for security tokens and ICO (Initial Coin Offering) for utility coins.

Crypto tokens gain value through their roles, features, and purpose.

- **Roles** include the rights of the token holder within the ecosystem (rights to vote, etcetera), value exchange (buy or sell tokens), toll (gateway to enable functionalities), function (enrich the experience of users), currency (store of value), and earnings (profits or financial benefits).

  For tokens to be considered valuable, they must possess more than one role.

- **Purposes** include bootstrapping engagement (right), economy creation (value exchange), skin in the game (toll), enriching the user's experience (function), seamless transactions (currency), distributing benefits (earnings).

- **Features** include product usage, governance, voting, ownership, contribution, product access (rights), work rewards, product creation, buying, spending (value exchange), running smart contracts, usage fees, security deposit (toll), an incentive for usage, connects with users, joining networks (function), transaction unit or payment unity (currency), benefit-sharing, profit sharing, inflation benefits (earnings).

The Howey Test

For tokens to be recognized as security tokens, they should meet the three criteria of the Howey Test. This test determines if the transaction will qualify as an 'investment contract' under the Securities Exchange Act of 1934 and Securities Act of 1993.

- The token represents an investment of money
- The token's investment is in a common enterprise
- There is an expected profit from the work of the third party or promoters

Meet the most important altcoins

Ether (ETH)

Ether is an Ethereum cryptocurrency and operates on its proprietary blockchain. It is second to Bitcoin in terms of market cap and the largest among all Altcoins. This coin is designed for the Ethereum network, but it is also accepted as payment by several online sites that sell services and merchants.

As a platform, Ethereum went live in July 2015 after programmer Vitalik Buterin talked about the idea in 2013. Together with Buterin who is serving as the public face and CEO is Joe Lubin of ConsenSys. It is responsible for the popularity of ICOs (initial coin offerings). It owns a programming language known as Solidity. Ethereum solidifies its position in the crypto world by introducing a programmable blockchain.

Its network serves as a melting pot for games, apps, and financial services, promising ultimate protection of accounts from theft, fraud, and censorship. It accepts Ether as payment for all transactions. As of January 2021, the market cap of ETH was $1,218.59 and a market cap of $138.3 billion.

By the end of 2030, the fearless forecast of Coin Price Forecast for Ethereum market value is $5,000.

Litecoin (LTC)

Litecoin was created by a former engineer of Google, Charlie Lee. It was launched in 2011 or just two years after bitcoin. It has a lot of Bitcoin's features, which is why people called it "a silver to Bitcoin's gold." Its software is faster than Bitcoin but almost the same.

It has a supply limit cap of 84 million. By 2023, it is expected to be 50% at its current 2 ½ minutes to mine a block.

The Litecoin Foundation projected that the last blocks will be mined around 2142. As of January 2021, it ranked as the world's 6th –largest crypto with a per-token value that amounts to $153.88 and a market cap of $10.1 billion.

The market value of Litecoin will hit $2,250 by 2030 according to the Crypto Research Report Group.

Binance Coin (BNB)

Binance coin is categorized as a utility cryptocurrency. It functions as a payment for trading and paying fees on the Binance Exchange. This altcoin was launched in July 2017, running with ERC-20 token in the Ethereum blockchain. Eventually, it is used as the proprietary currency of the Binance Chain, the decentralized blockchain of Binance. The man behind the creation of the Binance Exchange was Changpeng Zhao.

As of January 2021, one BNB was worth $44.26 with a market cap of $6.8 billion.

Coin Price Forecast believes that
Binance market value
by 2030 would reach $1,191.

Bitcoin Cash (BCH)

Bitcoin Cash is Bitcoin's spin-off during a hard fork in August 2017. This coin has its own unique blockchain and can process an average of 116 transactions every second. The original Bitcoin can only process 7 transactions per second. It was originally created with 8 MB blocks and eventually increased to 32 MB for better scalability.

Its primary function is to serve as a payment method or as a 'digital cash'. When it debuted on major exchanges, the opening market value of Bitcoin Cash was up to $900 and jumped to $4,091 during the end of 2017.

Bitcoin Cash aims to create a 21 million supply, just like Bitcoin. As of January 2021, the value per Bitcoin Cash was $513.45 and a market cap of $8.9 billion.

According to Digital Coin Price, the market value of Bitcoin Cash could reach up to $700 by the end of 2021.

Tether (USDT)

Tether is a dominant coin in terms of crypto trading. It is categorized as a Stablecoin and one of the most popular. It is actually the US dollar's tokenized version, making it very 'stable' in nature. Many people use Tether to hedge their assets against volatility and for liquidity. Tether coins are issued by Hong Kong-based Tether Limited.

Tether is a most-traded type of altcoin because it is cheaper, easier to use, and has lower transaction fees. About 75% of Bitcoin trading this 2021 is using Tether.

The market cap of Tether as of January 2021 was $24.4 billion and its token value was worth $1.

While the market price of Tether remains $1, Trading Beast forecast it would increase to $1.2817439 by the end of 2022.

Polkadot (DOT)

Polkadot is a unique cryptocurrency with translation architecture and has a heterogeneous multi-chain interchange. Behind the Polkadot are Peter Czaban, Robert Habermeier, and Gavin Wood. Wood is one of the co-founders of Ethereum. He wrote Polkadot's protocol, which is designed to link the blockchains (permission-less and permissioned) and oracles to form a relay chain that offers interoperability of the different networks.

It also allows the developers to generate their own blockchain using Polkadot's security measures. This concept is referred to as shared security.

As of January 2021, 1 DOT's market value was $12.54 and a market cap of $11.2 billion.

By 2030, Coin Price Forecast predicts that the market price of Polkadot would hit $41.81.

Cardano (ADA)

Cardano is dubbed as the 'killer of Ethereum' because its blockchain technology is more efficient. Behind this cryptocurrency is Charles Hoskinson, who left Ethereum after some disagreements with his other co-founders when he saw the direction it was taking. He co-founded this ouroboros proof-of-stake digital currency based on the research-based methodology.

The various research of the project was done by crypto experts, mathematicians, and engineers. Cardano's digital asset is ADA which is named after the English mathematician and 19th-century Countess Ada Lovelace.

As of January 2021, the trading price of 1 ADA was $0.31 with a market cap of $9.8 billion.

By 2030, Price Coin Forecast prediction for ADA's market price is $6.03.

Ripple (XRP)

Ripple is both a digital payment system and a cryptocurrency. The founders Jed McCaleb and Chris Larsen made it public in 2021. Its primary process is a remittance and payment settlement asset exchange. Its crypto token is XRP whose function is to act as an intermediary exchange mechanism between two different networks or currencies.

Rather than utilize the blockchain mining process, it adopts the consensus mechanism to confirm the transactions with the help of bank-owned servers. Transactions in Ripple are cheaper and faster. In the context of market capitalization, it was the 5th-largest altcoin with around $60 billion market capitalization and a market price of $1.60.

Coin Price Forecast for XRP's market price by 2030 would be $5.45.

Dogecoin (DOGE)

Dogecoin is the result of the collaboration of two software engineers Jackson Palmer and Billy Markus. They were joking about the cryptocurrencies' wild speculation and decided to make a payment system. That was a joke also, but some individuals saw it as a legitimate investment instrument.

On December 6, 2013, Dogecoin was launched to the public with Shiba Inu dog face as its logo. On May 5, 2021, the market cap of Dogecoin reached $85,314,347,523. It is the latest altcoin that achieved social media hype, thanks to Elon Musk, Gene Simmons, Snoop Dogg, and other known personalities.

> *In 2030, Dogecoin's market price would reach $17.50 according to the Cryptocurrency Price Prediction.*

Stellar (XLM)

Stellar Lumen is a cryptocurrency that was developed by Jed McCaleb and Joyce Kim in the early part of 2014. McCaleb was one of the founders of Ripple Labs and the developer of Ripple protocol. When he left Ripple, he collaborated with Kim and established the Stellar Development Foundation.

Lumens are traded using the blockchain-based Stellar network. The platform's distributed ledger system connects payment systems, banks, and users in low-cost, efficient cross-border transfers of values and payment purposes. Its shining moment happened in 2017 when lumens price soared more than 300 times.

As of January 2021, the market cap of Stellar was $6.1 billion and 1 Lumen is valued at $0.27

According to Coin Price Forecast, the market value of Lumen would be $1.39 by the year 2030.

Monero (XMR)

Monero is a private, secure, and untraceable cryptocurrency that was introduced to the market in April 2014. The open-source blockchain of Monero is opaque, disguising the users' addresses and making the transaction details including the amount anonymous. This total privacy is due to ring signatures.

As of January 2021, the market cap of Monero was $2.8 billion and the amount per 1 XMR amounted to $158.37.

Coin Price Forecast has predicted that by 2030, the market price of Monero would reach $1,006.

Tron (TRX)

Founded by Tron Foundation headed by its CEO Justin Sun, Tron uses the peer-to-peer (P2P) and blockchain components. To process transactions, it utilizes the proof-of-stake algorithms. It is also becoming a huge competition to Paypal and other payment processors because of its popularity among content consumers and content creators.

Its cryptocurrency is Tronix (TRX), which is worth $0.05 can be used to pay content producers and access what they are offering.In terms of market capitalization, TRX ranked 22nd in the March 2021 list of cryptocurrencies.

In 2030, TRX market price would hit $0.3048 according to

ZCash (ZEC)

ZCash is a crypto coin that provides what Bitcoin cannot- the option for the transactions to be viewed if the users allow it.

It means that they can protect their privacy by being un-trackable in the blockchain. The enhanced privacy features of this altcoin are due to the zk-SNARKs (Zero-Knowledge Proofs), which validate transactions without compromising the private details of the users.

It was introduced to the crypto market in October 2016 by its founder Zooko Wilcox-O'Hearn. The currency symbol of ZCash is ZEC. Its market capitalization is $1,145,782,989 with over $11 million in circulation.

Coin Price Forecast predicts that in 2030, ZCash market price would jump to $449.

NEO

NEO was founded in 2014 by Erik Zhan and Da Hongfei as AntShares but later rebranded into NEO. Its Onchain technology offers a centralized approach that enables 'dapps' or decentralized applications that generate smart contracts.

This is in line with their goal of creating a digital smart economy that delivers fast, secure, and seamless transactions.

And while the Chinese government still imposes restrictions on crypto transactions in the nation, NEO seems to be thriving well in the virtual ecosystem. It has a 3rd key feature that separates it from other blockchain-based cryptos – the digital identity.

NEO's base asset is the NEO token that creates GAS tokens. NEO has a market cap of over $2 billion. It has more than $70 million coins in circulation.

Watchlist: DeFi coins and tokens that are taking markets by storm

Decentralized finance or **DeFi** is an innovative method to execute various financial transactions with the help of apps. It is done over the blockchain, eliminating the traditional intermediaries (banks, exchanges, brokerages). DeFi uses smart contracts or code bits that process the transactions once the required conditions are met. Smart contracts self-execute once the expectations occurred.

In essence, DeFi is the concept that defines any transaction or application that uses cryptocurrency or blockchain technology in creating an alternative financial product. It offers a cheaper, faster option of digital peer-to-peer transactions with no minimum transaction amount. In 2020, DeFi tokens outperformed BTC. As of April 22, 2021, it has reached its TLV (total value locked) at $59.07 billion.

Here's a list of the top DeFi tokens that are showing incredible growth:

- **Uniswap (UNI)**

  The governance token and native currency of Uniswap is UNI. The crypto coins were first distributed to the users of the decentralized finance protocol. Each user that has utilized it before September 1, 2020, was given 400 UNI tokens ($1,400 worth during that time).

  Uniswap was a brainchild of the former Siemen's mechanical engineer Hayden Adams on November 2, 2018. It was popular among investors and traders because the protocol provides automated transactions using smart contracts mostly on the Ethereum blockchain.

  In terms of daily trading volume, Uniswap was the 4th overall 4th largest crypto exchange in October 2020. It generated $2-3 million in fees every day in March 2021. UNI's market cap is over $10 billion.

- **Chainlink (LINK)**

  Chainlink's token is Ethereum (ERC-677) based. As of January 2021, 1 LINK is worth $21.53 and has an $8.6 billion market cap. Chainlink is the industry's standard decentralized oracle network. It empowers smart contracts to access off-chain computation and real-world data in a secure manner. With the backing up of blockchain technology, Chainlink offers the utmost security and reliability.

It was established by Sergey Nazarov in 2017 and has garnered $32 million during its ICO (initial coin offering).

- **Maker**

Maker's TLV (total value locked) is $10 billion and has a market capitalization of 4.5 billion. It experienced its all-time high on April 22, 2021, with a $4,943.66 market price. It experienced its all-time low on January 30, 2017 with $21.06.

Maker is the MakerDao's governance token that holds the record of being the first blockchain-based protocol that started DeFi's booming market as well as the automated crypto-lending platforms. This token allows users to vote using the borrowing and lending system that creates the Stablecoin DAI, which is a community-managed cryptocurrency.

- **Compound (COMP)**

  After using the Ethereum network for 3 years, Compound finally launched COMP as its native token in June 2020. Its total value locked (TLV) is $9.5 billion with a market cap of $2.8 billion. It reached its all-time high of $612 on April 16, 2021.

  Its popularity in the crypto market is anchored on its borrowing and lending decentralized blockchain technology. Users earn interests or cTokens when they deposit their cryptocurrency in any of the Compound pools. The cTokens represent your C pool stake, so when you deposit Ether, you will be getting ETH. Moreover, for as low as 1% total COMP supply, you can vote for the proposals regarding the protocol change or submit your proposal.

- **Ankr (ANKR)**

  As of April 22, 2021, the market cap of Ankr was $1.05 billion with a limited supply that totals 10 billion. As of today, there are over 7 billion ANKR coins circulating in the market.

  This Ethereum token powers up the Web3 infrastructure of Ankr. It is a cross-chain staking platform that builds dApps and hosting nodes that enhance the blockchain ecosystem's efficiency. ANKR is used as payment for API services and node deployment.

- **Aave (AAVE)**

  Aave's protocol allows the users to act as a depositor or a borrower. It has interesting features that offer loans without collateral and flash loans. The protocol also stores digital funds on non-custodial smart contracts of the Ethereum blockchain. AAVE token comes with a voting right to improve the protocols and participate in governance. It reached a $668 all-time high price on May 18.

- **Mantra Dao (OM)**

  The native token of Mantra Dao is OM, which provides full voting rights for the users. This community-based DeFi platform focuses on governance, lending, and staking. The token holders govern the ecosystem and are given rewards for their positive contributions. This is through Karma, which is the system's reputation mechanism (works the same as credit scores). Mantra Dao is utilizing the public blockchain Riochain, which is both secure and scalable.

- **Coti Network (COTI)**

COTI's reputation has been moving upward consistently since May 24, 2021, when it sparked a bullish engulfing candlestick. This DeFi platform helps various organizations build their own payment systems and digitize their own cryptocurrencies.

Its crypto is categorized as DAG or directed acyclic graph. It does not need miners and blocks to use blockchain. It uses the consensus algorithm Trustchain which allows one-click requests for payment purposes, uses trust scores when confirming transactions, and utilizes smart contracts.

Other interesting developments include the integration of margin trading in the platform, the release of credit card processing solution Paywize, and the long-overdue integration with partner Celsius.

- **Serum (SRM)**

The native token of Serum is SRM, which has a 10 billion maximum supply. Ten percent of the total supply was already unlocked during its first year, while the remaining ninety percent will be unlocked within the 7-year period. About 50 million tokens are already circulating in the crypto sphere.

The decentralized ecosystem and exchange offer a very fast and low fee in processing transactions. Working on the SOL or Solana network, it can make 50,000 transactions every second.

- **Beam (BEAM)**

  BEAM tokens have a total value of $21.9 million as of December 2020. Currently, its trading price is between $0525 and $0.96. The Beam is a private DeFi platform that guarantees safe, quick, and anonymous transactions.

  It is utilizing two protocols- LelantusMW and Mimblewimble. They work together in creating smart contracts between crypto users without a third party. All transactions do not show private information on the blockchain, making them private by default.

	Key Point
	When trading crypto, always treat it as a part-time or full-time business and not a job or a hobby.

Why you should trade altcoins

The breakthrough success and its decade-old staying power in the crypto market make alternative coins more attractive to people who want to start small and test the trading game.

History showed that during the Bitcoin bull cycle in 2014, its previous $250 all-time high reached $1,200. During that time, the market value of Litecoin hit $50. Bitcoin soared again when Elon Musk invested $1.5 billion, creating a new all-time high. Again, the price surge benefitted the altcoins.

Many crypto experts are predicting that 2021 can be an altseason or year of altcoins. Altcoin season is an exciting period for altcoin holders because of the lucrative opportunities to gain substantial profits. The most notable Altseason happened in December 2017.

Other reasons:

- You can start small or just with $100 and gain a 100% to 1,000% return.

- Crypto is the future. It literally alters the future of the payment system, trading, investing, and more. And technology keeps innovating and transforming every single moment.

- As Bitcoin grows stronger, altcoins follow.

- There is thrill and fun in riding the crypto waves- the phenomenal gains and the dramatic lows. While there are risks, the promise of profiting from altcoin trading is exciting.

- Getting started in altcoin trading is easy. Once your account is verified and activated, you are in. Trading does not need huge capital, qualifications, or experience.

How to trade altcoins?

To begin trading altcoins, you first need to register an account. Registration is open and free to any interested trader. Study the different available exchanges and select the one that matches your goals and expectations.

- Accomplish the online form with the necessary information which typically requires name, contact number, email address, and password.

- The system will send a verification message to your email address and you need to press the link to activate your trading account.

- Invest an initial amount as your trading fund.

- Buy your altcoins and start trading.

- Monitor your profits/losses.

- Know when to sell your altcoins.

- Cash out.

If you are still testing the waters, you can try these investment strategies:

1. Buy & HODL
Holding out on your altcoin longer is always a safe and effective way. All you need is a reliable exchange and a crypto wallet to generate passive income. You can also buy just small fractions of coins or tokens to increase your crypto holdings.

2. Compound interests
Focus on creating a small percentage gain a day through compound interests. You can earn 10% every day for 30 days and double your initial investment
.

3. Follow the hype.
Remember that in altcoin trading exchanges, you are not competing with the hardcore Bitcoin traders, but more of the average traders.

4. Stake and save

Staking is a great way to support the ecosystem of the crypto network. It involves holding the tokens in a staking pool or a network to earn interest. The network will use the staked tokens for transaction verification and then paying a return.

Must-have altcoins to own before the altseason:

The Top Three

Ethereum (Ether)

This popular crypto coin was the first altcoin that drove the previous altseason. In 2018, it set a phenomenally high price for altcoins when it jumped to $1,500. At present, Ethereum is the world's second-largest cryptocurrency that gained over 450% growth in 2020.

Many are speculating that Ethereum can break the all-time high and hit $2,000 or more because of the following factors:

- o strong fundamentals

- o growing interest of the institutional investors

- o increased developer activities

- o infinite innovation potential of its ecosystem

- o store value as a payment unit

- o rise of DeFi

- o the launch of the Ethereum 2.0

Binance Coin (BNB)

In terms of market cap and market value, this coin is gaining significant growth since 2017, the year when it launched its own decentralized exchange BNB's success can be attributed to its cheaper fees and faster transaction process.

Litecoin (LTC)

Its parabolic cycle gives Litecoin momentum to rank 8th in the total market cap of the largest crypto. It has gained more than 250% growth in 2020 and is regarded as one of the must-have altcoins. Litecoin is known for its affordable and lightning-fast transaction speed.

The Runner-Ups

Bitcoin Cash (BCH)

This P2P altcoin offers relatively quick, low-cost cross-border transactions. It was created to become a good alternative for a more expensive Bitcoin transaction. This alternative coin is on the list of the top 10 cryptocurrencies in terms of market cap.

Tron (TRX)

Tron is continuing its journey to the top, becoming one of the most exciting altcoins to trade these forthcoming years. Its network shields user's data and privacy.

Moreover, it gained huge traction among content creators because they can easily monetize their digital works using TRX.

Fun Trivia

History shows that the largest ICO happened in 2017 when Filecoin collected its first $200 million in about 30 minutes and $257 million in total.

Altcoin trading guide for beginners

Are you excited to join the millionaires' club by trading Altcoins? Crypto trading is one of the easiest, but also the riskiest undertaking to earn your millions. So, how to profit from Altcoin trading? Preparation and understanding how it works are the keys to success.

1. Understand the dynamics of the cryptocurrency market.

While you are seeing people who are generating huge profits, many are losing significant amounts, too. Just like forex markets, the crypto markets operate in buying and selling assets. What makes altcoin trading highly volatile is the lack of regulatory rules because of its free operation model. But this volatility is viewed by traders as a profitable opportunity while mastering the strategies of winning.

2. Get yourself familiar with the 2 main trading strategies.

- Short-term strategy

  It refers to trading where traders hold the altcoins for weeks, days, hours, or even minutes. Holding the cryptocurrencies for several months can also be classified as short-term trading. Day trading is an example of a short-term strategy.

Pros

- High-return opportunity – Prices of altcoins can swing overnight or double in a few hours.

- 24/7 trading – This strategy does not conform to the U.S. Pattern Day Trading Rule that prohibits traders with below $25,000 balance in their accounts to trade more than three days a week.

Cons

- Higher volatility – The market prices of Altcoins change swiftly due to their volatile nature.

- Requires big investment to gain huge returns – Beginners who lack the financial muscle to trade consistently despite some losses along the way will lose the shining opportunities. Another factor is the lack of confidence or fear of losing lots of money.

- Long-term strategy

  Traders who use this technique buy altcoins and hold them for a certain period like 1 year or until the price has grown considerably.

  Pros

  - Easy trading – All you need to do is to buy and hold your cryptocurrency as long as you want. You don't need to stress yourself by monitoring the price movement constantly and looking for windows of opportunity to sell your altcoins.

  - Does not require a lot of money to start trading- This strategy lets you buy altcoins progressively to expand your investment portfolio.

  Cons

  - Missing quick gain opportunities – Price rises and falls within short periods regularly, so you miss the golden chances to earn profits

when you opt for a long-term
strategy.

3. Anticipate the Altseason

During this season, traders do not preserve or
hold altcoins. Instead, they seize the
opportunities to reap large rewards. There is a
buzz of positive anticipation in the air as the
value of altcoins starts to rise.

Investors and traders become more active in the
virtual sphere, accumulating more crypto or fiat
to maximize their chosen trading or investing
strategies.

Here are some tips to optimize the benefits of
the next altseason:

- Learn the meaning of Bitcoin dominance

  Bitcoin dominance simply means that
  Bitcoin has a larger market share
  percentage. It is characterized by the
  number of traders holding or selling their
  BTC. As the number spikes, the bitcoin's
  market cap also surges and negatively
  impacts the altcoin's market value.

  But when this dominance of bitcoin drops
  and holders begin to sell their BTC, the
  value of altcoins will soar. This is the
  onset of the much-anticipated altseason.
  It is typical during this period for bitcoin

owners to exchange their assets for alternative coins or fiat currency.

This is an excellent time to dispose of your long-term altcoin holdings because many investors would prefer to buy altcoins instead of BTC.

- Make sure that you are using the right tools

  The right investment or trading tools will make your journey in the crypto market much easier and provide better outcomes. It is necessary to invest in the most efficient and effective tools to help you as a beginner.

  And because the altseason does not stay for long, it is crucial to use a trading app or crypto exchange that will give your profits every time there is a price fluctuation.

  What are these tools? They refer to portfolio balancers, portfolio managers, crypto news aggregators, market watchers, charts, electronic wallets, trading apps, and trading exchanges.

- Do not FOMO

  FOMO or fear of missing out always brings a snowball effect, spiking the prices of altcoins. When people sense that the altseason is on the horizon, the majority is afraid to be left out so they invest more, resulting in the spiraling of altcoins' market value to the top.

As a beginner, do not live in FOMO to avoid costly mistakes. While losing is part of the trading journey, it's best to delve deeper and learn how the crypto market can work to your advantage. Do not just rely on your instincts. Learn and master the best techniques that can help you gain more.

- Always take your profits

  Be smart and sell your altcoins when the bitcoin dominance is declining.

  During this period, the prices of altcoins are at their peak. Do not miss the chance of profiting significant gains by holding on to them longer. Some traders hold on longer thinking that the momentum will continue, then get surprised when the market displays a sudden retracement.

- Diversify your portfolio

  As the cliché goes, "Never place all your golden eggs in a single basket." This means diversifying your portfolio with altcoins that are showing great potential as winners. To know which are the best ones to trade, always conduct technical and fundamental analyses. Altcoin diversification helps you avoid many losses when one or two of your crypto coins/tokens do not perform well. You can still break even or gain profits from other performing altcoins in your portfolio.

Beginners' trading mistakes that you should avoid

- Never trade what you cannot afford to lose.

- Do not take unnecessary risks, trade wisely.

- Do not be greedy when you start making money in trading. Take out your profits whenever possible.

- Don't chase 1,000% and live in FOMO.

- Make your own decisions based on technical and fundamental analysis, not because of others' opinions. Stop living in fear, uncertainty, and doubt (FUD).

- Don't fall in pump and dump or when the altcoin prices are inflated by trader's groups.

- Avoid making an emotional decision or panic buying and selling altcoins.

- Set stop loss to protect your gains.

- Higher potential for fraud and scams

TRIVIA

Namecoin (NMC) was launched on April 18, 2011, considered the first altcoin. It is now a dead coin after a 7-year history. NMC has been credited for showing that there is space in the crypto world other than Bitcoin.

FAQs

Can I cancel my altcoin trade that has not been fulfilled yet?

Yes. To cancel your trade order, simply press the system's "CANCEL" button. Once the cancellation is processed, your payment will be credited back to your trading account.

Is there a fee for canceling a trader order?

You don't need to pay fees for canceling trade orders.

What if I make a trading error, is it possible to reverse it?

No. All trades are final and irreversible.

Chapter 7

Best Exchanges for Bitcoins and Altcoins

In the general context, exchange refers to the marketplace where financial instruments, commodities, derivatives, and securities are traded for profits. Its core function is to provide a venue for orderly and fair trading transactions. It disseminates updated price information and other details of the trading assets.

An exchange is a platform where individuals, companies, groups, or government entities sell securities or stocks to interested investors to raise capital.

At a glance

- ✓ **What is a crypto exchange?**
- ✓ **How does it work?**
- ✓ **Top exchanges to check out**
- ✓ **Other trading exchanges to consider**
- ✓ **Frequently Asked Questions (FAQs)**

What exactly is a crypto exchange?

To jumpstart your trading journey, you need a place to buy altcoins. The kind of altcoin you wish to access is determined by the trading platform you select. With hundreds of choices, you need to be smart in the selection. The best exchange for you has the features and the crypto coins or tokens you want to invest in.

A crypto exchange or DCE (digital currency exchange) allows people to trade cryptocurrencies to own other digital currencies or fiat money. It can be a matching platform or a market maker. The first type matches the needs of buyers and sellers and charges transaction fees. A market maker exchange provides bid-ask spreads and gets commission for rendering its service.

How does it work?

In the crypto business, exchanges are essential.

- They send coins to the digital wallets of users.
- They facilitate trading transactions.
- They transfer profits to the accounts.

- They offer conversion of cryptocurrency balances into fiat currency using anonymous prepaid cards, allowing users to withdraw funds using ATMs anywhere in the world.

Some crypto exchanges allow altcoin-bitcoin pairs or buy/sell altcoins using BTC. It works well for traders who like tracking the performance of their investment portfolio against Bitcoin-the king of cryptocurrency.

Other exchanges offer interest-bearing accounts, financial derivatives, or pre-approved lending.

Satoshi Nakamoto Quote

"Lost coins make everyone else coins worth slightly more."

Top crypto exchanges to check out

Crypto exchanges support different kinds of altcoins. This is why you need to weigh the pros and cons of every option.

It is also important to review the transaction fees, coin availability, trading volume, security measures, and ease of use of the platform.

Let's take a look.

Binance: The best exchange for traders

Binance offers the widest range of altcoins. It supports 184 cryptocurrencies and tokens, 591 trading pairs, and more than 150 payment methods.

Binance also offers financial derivatives and allows margin trading for those who want to leverage their cryptocurrency positions.

It is the leading exchange that allows a variety of trading choices: altcoins against Bitcoin, altcoins against the U.S. dollar or other fiat currency, and USDT trading pairs.

Features and benefits:

- Has various tools for efficient trading
- Peer-to-peer crypto trading with zero fees

- 24/7 customer service
- Compatibility with Web, PC, and iOS or Android devices
- Delivers an average daily trading volume of 1.2 bn or over 1,400,000 transactions in every second
- Offers both advanced or basic trading exchange interfaces
- Has supporting services that allow users to transact using digital currency
- Provides an electronic wallet to store the virtual funds
- Offers programs to traders to make intelligent investment decisions and program for miners
- VIP program that frequently offers discounts and rewards

Binance is also known for offering the lowest fees for transactions. You can use their native token Binance coin (BNB) to pay transaction fees and get a discount. Binance does not charge fees for fund deposits, only when you withdraw your balances.

TRADING ON BINANCE

Before you trade your altcoins on Binance, you need to be aware of minor details that can impact your trading success. This includes fees, security measures, and possible taxes. In terms of fee, the exchange charges a flat fee of 0.1% to execute both buying or selling cryptocurrency. You get to pay the transaction fee once your order is fulfilled.

- If you are using another wallet, you need to transfer your altcoin to the Binance wallet.
- Once you have the fund, you can sell your altcoin for Bitcoin or Ethereum.
- If you're buying, set a market order (instant purchase or sell at current price) or a limit order (lets you enter/exit at a certain price point).
- Choose your base currency (the mainstream crypto that you wish to trade) for BTC or ETH.
- Pick the altcoin you want to sell (for example Stellar, EOS, or BNB) by tapping the ticker that opens up to the market page of the coin.

- Add your chosen altcoins to Favorites by tapping the star that is located in the upper right corner of the page for easy tracking.
- If you use a limit order, you need to tap the 'Order Book' on altcoin's market page. Input the price you wish to offload your crypto coin for and the quantity, then execute trading by tapping the red button 'Sell'.
- If you are utilizing the market order strategy, simply tap the 'Market Trades' in your altcoin and press the green button 'Sell'. After entering the quantity, tap the red button 'Sell' to execute your trading transaction. Binance will automatically convert the altcoin to ETH or BTC.

Coinbase: The best exchange for beginners and earning rewards

Coinbase is a friendly exchange for newbies who want to explore the potentials of cryptocurrencies. It was initially created for Bitcoin trading but eventually evolved to include altcoins and tokens to suit its decentralized nature. Now, it has more than 50 altcoins you can choose from. This online platform can be used for transferring, storing, buying, and selling digital currency. It supports over 100 countries that allow crypto transactions.

Features and benefits:

- provides an advanced trading platform to track your digital currency
- offers staking rewards
- provides an app that is compatible with Android and iOS mobile
- offers a digital wallet for retail investors and traders
- allows users to schedule their trading (daily, weekly, monthly)
- provides a custodial account for institutions
- has own stable coin that is backed-up by the U.S. dollars
- allows automatic conversion of one type of altcoin into another altcoin
- offers multiple investment options for institutional and individual clients
- has a Coinbase Earn account option where you receive crypto assets after watching educational videos
- allows fund deposits using a bank account, debit card, or credit card
- offers phone support and great customer service

- allows setting up of two-factor authentication for tighter security
- stores 98% of customers' money in cold storage
- low withdrawal and trading fees

Coinbase offers two other options:

- Coinbase Prime – It is designed for high-net-worth individuals and institutions. Individual accounts should have at least a $1 million deposit. Institutionalized clients gain access to the Asset Hub (where issuers can list and grow assets), cold or offline storage, and commerce services.

- Coinbase Pro – It is specially created for advanced traders. It allows users to access features like real-time order books, charting tools, and secure trading bots.

TRADING ON COINBASE

Log in to your account to check your portfolio balance and the performance of your crypto in time frames.

- To purchase altcoin, tap the 'Buy crypto' button above the portfolio balance. Enter a market order and a dollar value for the coin you want to buy. The button also gives you an option to set up a recurring order, convert crypto, or sell it.

- Check the page's top-right section to see the Send and Receive options. The action lets you transfer crypto by withdrawing funds from your Coinbase wallet or receive crypto via the virtual wallet.

Coinbase trading rules

- Every Trader's Account has a list of available Order Books. It settles trades in Fiat Currency and Digital Asset Trading Pairs.
- Users can place a Market Order, Stop order, or Limit Order. You can still cancel your order before it is fulfilled. Coinbase does not charge a fee for canceling orders.
- Traders who will try placing an Order to partially or completely fill more than 2% of the last trading price would receive a slippage warning.

- All types of Orders are subject to minimum and maximum size requirements.
- Traders are subject to Price-Time Priority or the time when the Taker Orders are posted.
- Both Coinbase Prime and Coinbase Pro charge a Taker Fee and a Maker Fee. Fees are calculated based on the quantity of the Order and charge in the Quote Asset.
- All Coinbase Trades are final and irreversible.
- Traders are not allowed to act as both takers and makers. Any attempt results in the cancelation of both Orders or self-execution.

Gemini: The best exchange for mobile users

Gemini has versatile features that work excellently for mobile users. It has a reliable mobile app for Android and iOS, letting you manage or monitor your crypto wherever you are. It is a fully regulated cryptocurrency exchange, offering bitcoin and other cryptocurrencies. This privately-owned exchange was introduced by Cameron and Tyler Winklevoss in 2015.

Features and benefits:

- has its own currency- the Gemini stablecoin
- allows users of the exchange to sell, buy, store, and trade crypto
- has a user-friendly mobile app and platform

- has an interest-paying savings account that gives users up to 7.4% balance interest
- has a payment app
- will have a Gemini credit card sometime in 2021
- offers up to 0% discount for volume traders
- operates 24/7, except during occasional maintenance window
- offers various options of limit orders like the IOC (immediate or-cancel), MOC (maker or-cancel), and AO (auction-only)
- is duly licensed by the NYDFS (NY State Department of Financial Services) to provide custodial services

- offers options for big institutional clients to have a segregated custody account that uses the Cold Storage system
- offers fee-free for extremely high-dollar transactions and separate fee structures for its mobile app, Active Trader, and Gemini Exchange offerings
- allows users to use a bank account to deposit and withdraw their funds

TRADING ON GEMINI

The interface of Gemini has a simple design that makes placing an order and trading convenient, even for beginners.

- To accumulate coins, find Buy on the Gemini's menu bar and select the crypto you wish to have.
- Check your remaining fund near the top of your computer or mobile screen. It shows both in bitcoin value and US dollar value.
- Review the total amount of your purchase together with the transaction fee before confirming your purchase. To complete the process, click Buy.

- To sell your altcoin, the process is the same. Select Sell and then input the quantity of coin you like to sell.

For more advanced traders, Gemini has the ActiveTrader. It features a block trading technique, multiple order types, advanced charting, and auctions. It can process and execute crypto trades in microseconds, with no security or reliability compromises.

ActiveTrader also provides order book visibility and has trading pair selectors that let you maximize the trading opportunities. It is optimized for smartphones and other mobile browsers.

eToro: The best exchange for active cryptocurrency traders

eToro is a social media trading platform for beginners. It was initially created as a forex platform that later on adapted the necessary tools for trading cryptocurrencies. This makes it excellent for active traders in both fields.

It eliminated the withdrawal for all U.S. clients, but still imposed a $5 fee for customers from other countries. Moreover, all U.S. traders can trade crypto in registered states.

Features and benefits:

- allows 24/7 trading of 15 cryptocurrencies
- has a unique feature CopyTrader, which allows the users to imitate the popular portfolio of traders by allocating a part of their funds and copy the way they trade
- comes with an easy-to-navigate, graphical interface and advantageous features
- allows traders to communicate ideas to help each other

TRADING ON eTORO

eToro's trading system requires manual input. Its capability to do social copy trading in real-time makes it a popular trading platform.

- To make money in eToro, you need to make the right choices such as keeping average loss smaller against average profit or taking risk-management decisions.

- When copy-trading, analyze the database of traders and decide what to copy, set maximum draw-down threshold, and how much funds to budget for each provider.
- Open leveraged or short positions with the help of CFDs.
- Opt for eToro long-term investment option which is CopyPortfolio. This concept bundles different financial assets or top traders into one investment instrument.

It has 3 types – Market Portfolio (finance, tech, gaming), Partner Portfolio (created by financial institution partners), and Top Trader Portfolio (traders with best practices).

CEX.IO: The exchange that offers the best cryptocurrency selection

CEX.IO is a crypto exchange that supports global traders in 48 US states and about 99% of countries in the world. It has over 80 crypto coins and tokens. It supports frequency trading and scalping to get data and assets.

Features and benefits:

- traders to use PayPal Debit MasterCard, MasterCard, and Visa card
- has 'instant buy' feature (exclusive for debit and credit cardholders)
- offers crypto-backed loans and staking rewards
- has a mobile app for traders on-the-go
- provides spot trading and margin trading accounts for more advanced traders
- uses taker/maker schedule that is based on a 30-day trading volume
- allows users to trade on the margin platform with over 100 times leverage without securing another account
- provides downloadable reports that show transaction history and real-time account balances
- is registered in different locations across the world as a money transmitter business
- PCI DSS (Payment Card Industry Data Security Standard) compliant
- stores the users' funds on digital wallets that are locked in secure vaults

TRADING ON CEX.IO

There are 4 levels of trading accounts in CEX.IO. The account you get depends on the verification requirements you presented. The basic account can buy up to $2,000 worth of bitcoin and altcoins per month.

Verified accounts require an ID, driver's license, passport, proof of residency, and a selfie holding your valid identification card. You get the chance to purchase up to $100,000 worth of coins every month.

The last two accounts which are Corporate and Individual Business allow holders to buy unlimited amounts of coins.

Using a mobile app:

- To buy altcoins, go to the Trade page.
- Use the Limit Order or Market Order to place your order.
- Go to the screen top to change the currency and click your preferred pair button,
- Click 'Buy' to view the amount of the crypto coin you will get based on the present exchange rate. After agreeing to

the conditions, click 'Buy' again to complete your transaction.

- If you are using Market Order, your purchased coin will instantly be added to your account balance. If you are selling your altcoin using this order, enter the amount, tap the 'Sell' button, and confirm your action.
- To track your CEX.IO, open the Trade Pro History page.

Crypto.com: The best exchange for DeFi Exchanges

Crypto.com is one of the most secure and fastest exchanges that allow users to trade, transfer, or store more than 90 types of cryptocurrency. It has its own coin- the CRO or Crypto.com coin that offers more benefits as users stake more. It is both a crypto trading and payment platform.

It has a DeFi wallet, which is a non-custodial e-wallet that allows access to DeFi services, gives you total control of your keys, lets you farm and swap DeFi token, stake CRO to boost up to 20x yield, earn interests without lock-up terms, and send cryptocurrency at your chosen network fee and confirmation speed. It supports over 30 cryptocurrencies and stable coins.

Features and benefits:

- offers lower trading fees
- provides more rewards and interests on crypto deposits
- has a maker-taker pricing structure that rewards clients with greater trading volumes
- offers multiple ways to users who want to earn digital coins/tokens
- has a Crypto.com Visa Card that lets you spend your coins anywhere in the world where Visa is acceptable and earn an 8% interest
- offers 24/7 customer support
- has high liquidity
- offers 3x leverage in margin trading
- offers up to 50x leverage and ultra-low latency in derivatives trading

TRADING ON CRYPTO.COM

Once your account is up, you can transfer funds and begin trading.

- Check Balances using the top right button on the navigation menu to view the list of coins and tokens you can choose to deposit.
- Simply tap the 'Deposit' button to the address where you need to deposit the crypto.
- To withdraw funds, click the 'Withdraw' button. You have the option to transfer fiat currency to the app or withdraw funds from your external wallet.

- The simple interface of the platform is easy to use. On the left side, you can view the trading chart. On the right side, the types of orders and order books can be seen. To monitor the performance, check the chart below.
- To open a trade position, go to the Markets on the top left section of the navigation bar. Choose the market you wish to trade in and the pair you want to trade. Select Trade and input the necessary information on the fields.
- Crypto.com exchange uses a market order and a limit order. Market order

simply involves specifying the amount of crypto you wish to purchase and it will be executed at the order's book best possible rate. On the other hand, when you use a limit order, the transaction will be filled once it reaches the lower price.

- There are no deposit and withdrawal fees in Crypto.com, only the on-chain transaction cost. Moreover, the more trades you do, the fewer transaction fees you will pay.

BitSquare: The best decentralized exchange

BISQ or BitSquare is a decentralized exchange, which means that the exchange does not hold your funds and there is no authority controlling the network. It uses a Multisignature wallet that asks for the seller, buyer, and independent arbitrator signatures.

Features and benefits:

- allows anonymous trading

- good list of altcoins and fiat currencies, including the rare ones
- has over 20 payment options like cash deposit, SEPA, bank transfer
- no deposit and withdrawal fees
- offers peer-to-peer trading, so you just need to pay the blockchain transaction fee
  depending on the amount you wish to trade
- buyers and sellers also need to pay arbitrator and holding fees
- excellent security
- easy-to-use interface and charts with trading information

TRADING ON BITSQUARE

The main characteristic of BISQ is decentralization, so each transaction is completely unique.

- To prevent cheating, it requires traders to deposit a security amount of 0.1 Bitcoin and 2 Bitcoins from the arbitrator. In return, the arbitrator earns a fee for successful transactions.

- An arbitrator will be selected randomly to be the third signature holder, adding security to every trading transaction.
- The system will place the coins to be sold and holding fees in the MultiSig wallet and lock them up until the deal is successfully confirmed.
- You can trade any of the altcoins available on the platform.

Kraken: The best exchange for margin and futures traders

Kraken supports more than 50 cryptocurrencies and traders in approximately 200 countries. It is one of the great exchanges for futures and margin trading as well as OTC trading. Its basic and user-friendly platform interface is perfect for beginners. It is a top choice of European traders for altcoin trading. Users who live in most parts of the European Union, U.S., Canada, and Japan can use their bank account for fund deposits and withdrawals.

Features and benefits:

- offers wider options for institutional and retail investors
- global trading and investing support
- has margin accounts that allow users to borrow up to 5x the crypto balance
- allows futures trading for Bitcoin, Litecoin, Ripple, Ethereum, and Bitcoin Cash
- offers staking rewards
- has a mobile app that is compatible with iOS and Android devices
- provides educational resources
- high-net-worth and institutional clients have access to Kraken's account management and consultation services
- trading fees can be as high as 0.26% or low as 0.02%
- offers live chat support

TRADING ON KRAKEN

Once your account is up, you can transfer funds and begin trading.

- The fastest way to sell, buy, or convert crypto in Kraken is using the 'Buy Crypto' button.
- Choose your preferred currency pair (ETH for US dollar or BTC to Euro) from the quote/ticker bar on the Trade page.
- Next, fill out the New Order form and choose whether to use a Limit Order or a Market Order.
- Submit your order and click the large Sell/Buy button. You can double-check the order in the confirmation screen (or skip it by checking a box).

- If you select the Market Order, the trade is instantly executed. Limit Order requires a short waiting period.

Bittrex: The best exchange for account security

Nothing beats Bittrex in the context of security. Along with its two-factor authentication, it keeps funds in cold storage using a multi-stage wallet method. Moreover, the transaction fees are lower than other exchanges. Its trading engine is designed for speed and scalability, providing real-time order execution.

Features and benefits:

- withdrawals and deposits of US dollars are free of charge
- imposes small network fee for crypto withdrawals
- uses maker/taker fee based on the unit of assets you trade in a month or trading volume
- has Instant Buy/Sell feature

- compatibility with Android or iOS mobile devices

TRADING ON BITTREX

Once your trading account is activated, you can begin trading. Check the Bittrex markets to find your base currency- Bitcoin Market, Ethereum Market, and USDT Market.

- Deposit the cryptocurrency you purchased into your Bittrex account. It will serve as your base currency to purchase the altcoins you want.
- Set up your Buy Order by adding the quantity of altcoin you desire to buy and the amount or price you want to spend.
- If you are off-loading your altcoins, set up a Sell order. Select the amount of crypto you wish to sell and the price you want for them.
- Confirm your transaction.

Poloniex: The exchange with a huge list of altcoins

This U.S.-based crypto exchange was established by Tristan D'Agosta in 2014 and has a high trading volume and liquidity. One downside of Poloniex is not supporting fiat currencies. It requires you to buy cryptocurrency to fund your trading account.

Features and benefits:

- deposits and withdrawal of funds are both free, only blockchain fee
- trading fees depend on the amount you spend – 0.25% to 0%
- good customer service, which includes live chat
- 24/7 support team to answer your concerns and resolve issues
- various trading tools like graphs and charts
- excellent security system
- big selection of altcoins
- user-friendly platform that works well for beginners and experienced traders
- allows users to access airdrops or distribution of crypto coins or tokens
- the app lets you connect with banks and cards
- lets you run bot trading strategies and smart algorithms
- allows you to do margin trading using a wide range of crypto pairs for bigger profits
- helps you earn without active trading through soft staking or P2P lending
- easy-to-use interface and charts with trading information

TRADING ON POLONIEX

Poloniex has everything you need to begin trading.

- Use your bank account, debit card, or credit card to purchase or sell your cryptocurrency.
- Trade your crypto assets with about 25 margin trading pairs and more than 200 spot trading pairs.

- Trade Poloniex Futures and leverage your crypto assets with up to 100x
- Earn rewards by joining trading campaigns

To trade either on a mobile device or desktop computer:

- Deposit funds on your trading accounts.
- Pick your preferred coins from the market tabs. Each tab offers a variety of coins and tokens with their current prices.
- Buy or sell your altcoin based on your selected trading pair. Input the number of coins and your desired price. You can do

it in 3 ways – manual entry, select from the Order book, or select the lowest ask price.
- Complete your transaction by hitting the 'Buy' button.
- Once the order is filled, it will be part of the Trade History.

Other trading exchanges to consider:

- **Coinmama**

  With over a 2 million customer base, Coinmama is a solid cryptocurrency exchange. It accepts all types of currency for payment and caters to high-end investors. It supports SEPA transfers for European users, SWIFT transfers for customers anywhere in the world, and Faster payment transfers for its UK clients

  Coinmama is not for casual investors or hobbyists. It requires $100 and $200 buy and sell limits. It has a good crypto selection that is available for direct purchase only and a small rotating number of altcoins that can only be exchanged with one another. In terms of transaction fees, Coinmama follows a loyalty system to determine the amount to pay. It does not impose fees for withdrawals and deposits.

- **Bitstamp**

Bitstamp was established in 2011 with features that work best for more experienced traders. It has the highest trading volumes with really good liquidity. This exchange allows users to use bank accounts, crypto, and credit/debit cards for trading and offers a low withdrawal fee for the Single Euro Payments Area (SEPA).

Trading fees for every transaction is 0.25% but go down when you spend over $20,000 in a single month. While it has Ethereum, Litecoin, Ripple, and Bitcoin Cash, Bitstamp does not offer a lot of altcoins. The verification process can take up to 2 weeks and the customer service is low. But it boasts of a range of trading tools for professional traders.

- **PrimeXBT**

This exchange lets traders use a single account to access multiple markets like cryptocurrencies, Forex, Commodities, and Stock Indices. PrimeXBT app supports iOS and Android platforms. It allows users to leverage their accounts to improve results and to respond quickly to changing market trends. Moreover, it allows users to copy the trading activity to get similar profits.

- **Overbit**

This exchange allows cryptocurrency and Forex trading. It allows users to leverage up to 100x on crypto and up to 500x on Forex. Other features that make Overbit attractive to traders include providing protection to your account against negative balance and limiting exposure with the help of advanced risk management.

The platform comes with a streamlined, minimalist design and keeps your fund in a MultiSig cold wallet. It allows opening and closing the trade position with ease and choosing margin allocation to prevent risks.

FAQs

How to select the best exchange?

The following factors can help you find the perfect crypto exchange for your trading style:

- platform's reputation
- security
- trading volume and liquidity
- ease of use and navigation
- transaction fees that it imposes on users
- delivery time
- customer support
- geographical location
- accessibility and restrictions
- transparency

What is the best and easiest way to buy coins and tokens?

The only way to do it is by choosing a secure, mature, and solid exchange that offers speedy trading.

Can I use more than one crypto exchange?

Absolutely yes. Having more than one exchange helps you diversify your assets. Each exchange has its own strengths and features that will help you trade more successfully.

Is it okay to transfer my crypto from one exchange to another?

Yes. To send you coins, simply go to your desired crypto exchange and find the deposit address. Now, go back to your source exchange and withdraw the number of coins you want to transfer to your target exchange address.

Are my cryptocurrencies safe on exchange?

As a rule, do not keep your crypto holdings on the exchange. While exchanges have security measures, there is always a possibility that your assets can be hacked. If you are an active trader, just leave the coins that you can afford to lose when the worst happens.

Take note that in 2020 alone, there were about 28 attacks on several exchanges. The largest of these cyber hacks happened in KuCoin, the Singapore-based exchange that lost over $200 million cryptocurrencies.

Do exchanges have insurance?

Some crypto exchanges offer insurance coverage to their customers to protect their digital assets against fraud or hacking. One example is Coinbase with a $255 million insurance policy that secures its reserves.

Why do crypto exchanges have different fee structures?

Exchange fees are typically charged for every crypto transaction. It differs when you are a buyer or a seller. Popular and bigger exchanges have higher fees due to the insurance coverage and added security measures. Other exchanges based the fees on trade percentage and price volatility. Also, different currencies charge different fees.

Why should I choose a popular exchange?

While there are exceptions to the rule, popular crypto exchanges have the highest trade volumes. Trading volume equates to great liquidity, which is an important factor when you want to trade, sell, or buy cryptocurrencies. When there are lots of trades, you can easily buy or sell altcoins at their best prices. An exchange with a low trade volume can cost you more. In terms of volume worldwide, the top 3 exchanges according to CoinMarketCap are Binance, Coinbase, and Huobi.

Why is user experience important when selecting an exchange?

An intuitive user interface provides a great user experience. This often leads to the quick growth of transaction volume. The value of exchanges is significantly tied to the number of users and transactions.

Chapter 8

The Quest for the Best Wallet

Altcoin wallets work like Bitcoin wallets. These digital wallets play a crucial role in the functions and growth of crypto coins and tokens. They serve as storage of holdings and make it convenient for users to transfer funds to each other.

While some altcoins have their own wallets, it becomes difficult in the long run to keep track of all your crypto assets. This is where you would be needing a single wallet that supports a variety of altcoins.

Technically, all wallets can hold more than one cryptocurrency. What makes them different from each other is the number of coins that they can store. Some of these multi-coin wallets can be selective, while other wallets serve as universal wallets.

At a glance

- ✓ **Why is it crucial to choose the best wallet?**
- ✓ **What are the fundamentals of the best altcoin wallets?**
- ✓ **Different types of cryptocurrency wallets**
- ✓ **Guide questions to ask yourself when choosing a wallet**
- ✓ **What I recommend: 5 best software wallets**
- ✓ **What I recommend: 5 best hardware wallets**
- ✓ **Exchanges with secure wallets**
- ✓ **Special mentions: Wallets with special features**
- ✓ **Custodial storage for High Net Worth Individuals (HNWI) and Institutions**
- ✓ **Frequently Asked Questions (FAQs)**

Why is it crucial to choose the best wallet?

The most important factor to consider when selecting a cryptocurrency wallet is security. It must have adaptive features that secure your funds and enable convenient transaction services. As more and more altcoins appear on the market, the number of altcoin wallets become also available.

While many of these digital wallets are designed specifically to provide security, there are others that are created as fronts for scams and fraud transactions.

This is why using the most trusted and the best altcoin wallet is important to avoid the trap of criminal activities and enjoy their perks.

Another factor is your purpose. If you are planning to buy and hold your altcoins for a certain period or long term, your best choice is a hardware wallet. In contrast, if you want to trade actively, a software wallet is the best option.

To limit the risk if you are using less secure platforms like exchanges, it is necessary to have a solid strategy. It means keeping most of your crypto assets in a hardware wallet or employing several wallets.

The safest way to store your funds is to keep them in a wallet that is not managed or owned by a third party (or exchange). It is important that only you know your private key to access your cryptocurrencies.

What are the fundamentals of the best wallets?

Choosing the best altcoin wallet requires careful review of their key features such as:

- Security - It is the most important characteristic of an altcoin wallet. Offline wallets or hardware wallets are more secure compared to online or web wallets. Wallets that use 2FA or 2-factor authentication are much more secure.

  If someone is trying to access your wallet, he still needs to go through the next level of verification which is entering the code that the system sends to your mobile phone. It prevents any unauthorized access to your funds.

- Control over your funds – Having full control and access to your coins offers peace of mind.

- Multi-currency – If you're planning or already have an array of crypto coins and tokens, a multi-currency wallet helps you store and manage them in a single storage.

- Multisignature – There are crypto wallets that act like joint bank accounts, requiring more than one signature to authorize transactions.

- Anonymity – If you value your privacy so much and want to trade without divulging personal information, consider a crypto wallet that offers this feature.

Cryptocurrency Wallets

A crypto wallet is a web-based application that stores the coins and tokens of users. Technically, your crypto does not leave the blockchain but is transferred to an 'address' that represents the wallet. The address is the 'specific location' of your account on the blockchain's network. Your wallet's public address is used by other crypto holders to send coins to your account. The crypto wallet stores your private keys so you can access your funds and send coins to others.

Crypto wallets are separate 'non-custodial' storage that gives you an option not to store your funds in the exchange's built-in wallets. They are also the necessary tool to interact with the blockchain of your preferred exchange or platform.

In essence, the function of these wallets is to generate the information needed to process and complete blockchain transactions.

It is important to never misplace or forget your 'seed' or recovery phrase. It refers to the string of random characters that will help you regain access to your cryptocurrencies in case that you forget your PIN code.

Types of wallets

Due to the continuous diversification of crypto strategies, a reliable and safe wallet for your altcoins is your must-have tool. Generally, they are classified into three types- software wallets, hardware wallets, and paper wallets.

1. Software wallets are app-based and need internet connectivity. When the wallet is connected to the internet, it is called a **hot wallet**.

This type of wallet is best for active users who generally store smaller amounts of funds. Hot wallets bring high utility but are less secure compared to cold wallets.

They can be subcategorized into:

- **Desktop wallet**

  This kind of wallet offers functions and features that protect your virtual fund against attacks and thefts. However, you need to download the entire blockchain of the altcoin on your computer before you can utilize it.

  After downloading it, you can access a special file that stores your private key. The key will unlock your altcoin wallet. Once you are in, you can perform crypto transactions like trading, buying and selling coins, and transferring funds anywhere in the world.

  A desktop wallet provides better security compared to a mobile wallet and web wallet. It's best to use a computer that you don't typically use or an older model of laptop with a clean operating system and completely offline. Just make sure you have a backup if the computer unexpectedly dies.

The popular choices among altcoin users are Exodus and Electrum.

- **Mobile wallet**

Mobile altcoin wallets are popular choices among on-the-go people who prefer to do transactions via their smartphones or other mobile devices. In essence, it is a mobile app that stores the users' private keys and allows access to their holdings whenever they need to perform transactions. It comes in handy when you need to pay for products or services of retail stores that are already accepting crypto payments.

The potential risks of using a mobile altcoin wallet include security threats and crypto thefts if you accidentally lose your phone or someone steals it.

Moreover, hackers target this type of wallet because it is the custodian of private keys, making it easy to access the holdings. This type of crypto wallet is prone to keyloggers, malware, and viruses.

Some of the most popular mobile wallets are Trust Wallet, Mycelium, Coinomi, Electrum, and Safepal.

- **Web wallet**

A web or online wallet is a cloud-based application that you can access using Google Chrome, Firefox, and other internet browsers. New users have to register on the app to get a private key and begin crypto transactions. Many people use this wallet because of its convenience and ease of use. It is the fastest way to complete your crypto transactions and does not lag between the server and app locations. It is ideal for storing small numbers of altcoins.

The downsides of this type of wallet include susceptibility to malware, DDOS attacks, insider hacking, and phishing scam. You may end up losing your funds because your private keys are stored online. If tonight the exchange is shut down or hacked, you will wake up without a single crypto coin.

To ensure higher security, always review the protective measures of the wallet to prevent loss of funds and breach in the system.

There are two kinds of web wallets – hosted and non-hosted.

- **Hosted wallets** hold the users' funds and private keys on the server. This type of crypto wallet is often the target of hackers, so make sure to review all the features of the wallets you are eyeing to. Providers of hosted wallets offer different levels of protection and are usually insured.

  Examples of hosted wallets are Binance, Coinbase, and CEX.io.

- **Non-hosted wallets** store your crypto assets but let you control your private key and seed words. This means that you have control over your funds and access it whenever you want.

Examples of non-hosted wallets are MetaMask and MyEtherWallet.

2. Hardware wallets are offline wallets with private keys that are embedded into the device that serves as storage of your coins and tokens. They are also called cold wallets because they are internet-dependent. These physical devices are the most secure way to store your coins.

They are ideal for users who like investing significant amounts of funds and those who like to trade their crypto once in a while to make a profit. To access your holdings and make transactions, you need to connect your hardware wallet to your laptop or desktop via Bluetooth or a USB port.

3. One variation of offline wallets is the **paper wallet**. It is a less technical wallet and works by generating a public address and a private key. Users need to print out the generated information on a piece of paper. Whenever you perform crypto transactions, you need to enter the private key in your software wallet.

To ensure safety, store the paper in a safe place or memorize the private key. Some paper wallet providers use QR codes to execute crypto transactions.

However, there are several flaws that make it a less popular choice like not being able to transfer partial funds to another user. Currently, paper

wallets are considered very risky, unreliable, inconvenient, and obsolete.

Do you know how to back up your crypto wallet?

The simplest way is to back up the seed phrases or wallet.dat files.
You can also create a QR code, print it, and store it in a safe place.
Another option is to copy the master key to the text file, encrypt it, and store the file in another wallet (preferably a hardware wallet).

Guide questions when choosing a wallet?

1. How should I select a wallet?

- If you are a beginner, you can start with a reliable online wallet that offers low fees for crypto transactions. Coinbase and Exodus are great choices.

- If you are already an experienced user, the best choice is a hardware wallet. It will be easy for you to navigate its added features. Ledger and Trezor are excellent options.

- If you are a serious crypto enthusiast, pick a crypto wallet with enhanced features and added security protocols. The best choices are Coinbase, Ledger, Exodus, and Trezor.

2. What are the top factors that you need to consider?

- *The kind of altcoin you want* - Some wallets support limited types of altcoins. The best altcoin wallet has hundreds of coins and tokens, providing an excellent experience that fits all.

- *How frequent are you going to trade* – If you are an active trader, the good option is a hot wallet because it allows you to buy or sell your altcoins wherever you are. If you are into long-term trading and investing, best to choose a cold wallet.

- *The price of the wallet* – Understand that while a hot wallet is free to set up, you need to pay a fee whenever you trade your crypto. A cold wallet or hardware wallet comes at a price but secures your crypto better.
- *The advanced features* – Innovative features like instant crypto conversion, real-time market insights, advanced reporting capability, tighter security protocols, and more always make a difference when choosing a wallet.

- *Peace of mind* – You should choose the type of wallet that will not give you anxiety over your virtual funds in terms of security and safety.

3. How secure are digital wallets?

The security features and protocols of individual altcoin wallets are extremely important to consider during the selection. It is your primary security tool, so it is crucial to make sure that the wallet will deliver the standard security features. Some wallets have sophisticated protocols when it comes to security matters such as utilizing the two-factor authentication process.

Others utilize biometrics during the validation process to keep the holdings safe. You may also consider subscribing to crypto custody services. This option offers recovery of lost coins caused by hacking. It is for crypto investors who prefer to use insured altcoin wallets and have no issues about having their private keys in the custody of the provider.

4. What level of accessibility does the altcoin wallet offer?

Accessibility is the wallet's capability to bypass varied geological barriers. This means that you can use it anywhere and anytime you need to do transactions. If you are a traveler, it's best to get a non-geo-selective altcoin wallet. Take note that the accessibility level of the crypto wallet is also determined by its classification. Mobile and online altcoin are best in terms of the accessibility of holdings.

5. How do the updates in the wallet help users?

Wallet providers continue to upgrade their products to resolve issues and loopholes in the system that hackers and thefts tend to capitalize on. It is important to check if your provider updates the system and its functionalities. This also speaks of the credibility of the wallet to protect your holdings. Look at how frequently they update the existing altcoin wallets and the convenience that the new features or improvements that it gives to users.

6. What are the added features that you should consider?

Providers of crypto wallets are now exploring ways other than just holding digital assets or securing the private keys of users. For one thing, the most popular wallets are now adopting innovative payment features, exchange tools, tracking tools, and a lot more.

Fun Trivia

Mt. Gox (Magic the Gathering Exchange) was the world's biggest exchange in 2014, handling about 70% of bitcoin transactions. But it went bankrupt after reporting the loss of 850,000 bitcoins.

What I recommend: 5 best software wallets

1. Coinomi Wallet

Coinomi is a very popular choice and trusted by millions of altcoin users. It is a Hierarchical Deterministic (HD), multi-chain, security-first wallet for both desktop and mobile users. Its security has never been compromised or hacked.

Pros

- supports over 1,700 crypto assets
- offers instant exchange of supported assets via the shapeshipt.io built-in exchange
- superb security protocols
- generates seed or protective phrase for the wallet
- offers greater anonymity/privacy
- offers free-of-charge services
- stores and encrypts the private key on the mobile device

Cons

- not open-source
- does not support fiat currencies
- not yet compliant with FCA or other crypto regulators

2. Exodus Wallet

Exodus is both a desktop and mobile crypto wallet that is best for altcoin traders. This free wallet can help you diversify your crypto portfolio and trade through their website or mobile app. It is sleek and very responsive, ranking high on the list of best altcoin wallets for beginners. Exodus allows you to purchase, exchange, or manage your altcoins in one single application.

Just remember that this wallet is non-custodial so it is up to you to safeguard your password and recovery phrase. You wouldn't want to lose your access to your holdings forever.

Pros

- a multi-currency desktop wallet that supports Windows, Mac, and Linux
- easy to set up, convenient to use, and free
- provides trading apps and live price charts

- supports more than one hundred coins and tokens
- intuitive interface
- encrypted, cold storage
- has a built-in shapeshift.io exchange that allows a single-click exchange of one coin/token to another crypto
- gets updated regularly (every 2 weeks)
- offers total control over the users' private keys and even encrypt them for them
- has advanced security protocols that keep hackers and malware threats away

Cons

- not completely open-source
- charges a higher conversion fee
- less secure compared to the hardware wallet

3. Guarda Wallet

Guarda is a universal, non-custodial altcoin wallet. It means that you need to secure the safety of your password as well as the recovery phrases. It is regarded as one of the excellent hot wallets for beginners and those with smaller holdings.

Pros

- works excellently on Windows, iOS, and Android systems
- comes with a dedicated Chrome extension (also with Linux, Mac, and Ubuntu app)
- free to set up
- easily connects to various partner exchanges
- very convenient to use
- offers private key access
- allows easy buying and exchanging of cryptocurrencies
- makes the process of fund transfer safer
- rewards crypto by holding coins

Cons

- supports a small number of cryptocurrencies (just over 50 coins and tokens)
- less secure than a cold wallet

4. Indacoin Wallet

Indacoin wallet is mobile-based, multi-currency storage that is available in both Android and iOS devices. This wallet allows users to exchange altcoins within the wallet. You don't need to move your crypto assets out to complete the process and help you manage the assets using one app.

Pros

- supports more than 100 crypto coins and tokens
- offers direct purchase or conversion of altcoins
- availability of recovery option
- allows you to buy altcoins using a credit/debit card and trade them
- easy to use and simple interface, which makes it perfect for beginners
- available in over 100 countries

Cons

- less secure because it only uses a 4-digit PIN
- Android app

5. Gemini Wallet

Gemini Wallet stores your assets safely in their institutional-grade cold storage and their insured hot wallet. The bulk of holdings are stored in the offline cold storage and easily accessible when needed by the users. It employs industry-leading infrastructure to ensure top-notch protection and security of the wallet. It is beginner-friendly.

Pros

- insurance coverage against Digital Assets theft (hot wallet)
- high-security storage
- continuous upgrade of wallet infrastructure to optimize users' experience and support new currencies
- offers native SegWit addresses
- easy-to-use
- 24/7 expert support
- availability in the 50 states of the U.S. and over 50 countries in Europe, Asia, Africa, Oceania, and South America

Cons

- restricted methods in buying and selling crypto (via bank or wire transfer only)

Did you know that?

Top 10 crypto exchanges typically earn around $62 million every month. Exchanges from the Top 50 earn an average of $26 million and Exchanges from the Top 100 earn $13 million.

What I recommend: 5 best hardware wallets

1. Ledger Wallets

Ledger is a popular choice when it comes to cold storage. This Paris-based company leveraged its proprietary technology in developing infrastructure and security solutions, including hardware wallets. Since its inception in 2014, Ledger wallets have sold over 1 million units in 165 countries and counting.

To ensure the highest standard of security protocols, Ledger uses BOLOS, a unique operating system that they integrate into the wallet's chip. Their flagship wallets are the bestselling Ledger Nano S and Ledger Nano S.

- **Ledger Nano S** accepts a variety of altcoins and ICO tokens. This hardware wallet comes with tamper-alert software that is perfect for both beginners and advanced users. You need to have it with you to ensure transaction approval. It also offers a desktop app called Live to offset the inconvenience and allows users to execute transactions or track them. It costs $59.

Pros
- supports over 1,100 crypto coins and tokens
- portable and lightweight
- easy to use
- offers excellent value
- sleek design
- powerful functionality
- highly-secure

Cons
- no private key access
- navigation can be inconvenient and confusing
- a bit complex setup and requires extra steps to buy or load crypto to the device
- not an open-source

- **Ledger Nano X** is a premium crypto wallet that stores your private key offline. It has all the features of Ledger Nano S and more. It can store more assets and lets you manage your portfolio while on the go via Bluetooth. You just need to link the device to your smartphone to access it. It is primarily designed for HODLers. It costs $119.

Pros

- o looks like a USB pen drive, making it easy to carry anywhere you go
- o offers extremely high security that is audited and verified by the French National cybersecurity agency ANSSI
- o employs custom build OS (BOLOS)
- o comes with CC EAL5 + certified Secure Element (SE) chip
- o has DeFi functionality
- o attractive design
- o offers a huge amount of space that can store up to a hundred applications
- o easy to use and set up

Cons

- o screen navigation is a bit complicated
- o more pricey
- o no private key access

2.Trezor Wallets

Trezor is a great choice when it comes to hardware wallets. It was built by SatoshiLabs, making it the first secure and legitimate wallet for

Bitcoin. Now, it caters to a large number of alternative coins and tokens. It comes with an OLED screen and looks like a tiny calculator.

All Trezor wallets come with a PIN code that is stored in the system. This eliminates loss of PIN even if the device or computer you use to access the wallet faces some technical issues.

Moreover, Trezor wallet features an inbuilt system that blocks brute-force attempts to access the funds. It works by raising the waiting time by a power of 2 for every incorrect input of the PIN code. Each wallet has a 24-word seed and passphrase that are RNG (Random Number Generator) selected offline and are displayed on the screen. You will be given new numbers in every transaction you do.

- **Trezor One**

    Pros
    - offers very secure offline storage
    - supports a large number of cryptocurrencies
    - supports Mac OS X, Windows, or Linux
    - simple to use
    - open source
    - sleek design

- o best for active traders and HODLers

Cons
- o on the more expensive side (costs $99)

- **Trezor T**

Pros
- o Colored touchscreen
- o very easy to use
- o extremely sleek design
- o compatible with Linux, Mac OS, and Windows
- o supports more coins and tokens

Cons
- o on the more expensive side (costs $159)

3.Prokey Optimum Wallet

Prokey Optimum is a good starter wallet for beginners because it is easy to use. But it is also a popular choice among advanced traders and investors who like its multi-functionality and high security. It costs $59.

Pros

- supports more than 1,500 coins and tokens
- compatible with Mac, Android, Windows, and Linux
- setup is easy
- connects easily with computers and mobile devices
- secure firmware that offers safety
- protects crypto assets from remote and physical hacks
- transparent and open-source
- Plug and Play

Cons
- small screen
- relatively new to the market

4.KeepKey Wallet

KeepKey is a robust hardware wallet that looks like a big phone or mini-tablet. It is a bit bulky and weighs about 55g. It supports more than 50 cryptocurrencies which include the most popular coins and tokens. This hierarchical deterministic (HD) wallet comes with a passphrase and PIN code. It costs $99.

Pros

- offers high security

- available on Windows, Mac, and Linux
- good value for your money
- large LCD screen
- integrated with ShapeShift
- well-built design

Cons

- no private key access
- has more user restrictions
- not pocket-friendly
- no Lock feature
- recovery seed is displayed only once

5.SafePal S1 Wallet

SafePal S1 is the first hardware wallet that Binance has invested in. Small as a credit card, you can take it anywhere you go.

Pros

- offers multiple layers of security sensor
- has a self-destruct mechanism
- 100% cold storage that does not require WiFi, Bluetooth, or USB connectivity

- supports more than 10,000 coins/tokens and 23 blockchains
- offers unlimited currency storage
- easy-to-carry and lightweight
- holds multiple crypto assets in a single device
- supports firmware upgrade

Cons

- made of plastic material, which makes it fragile

Exchange Wallets

Most crypto exchanges have built-in storage or exchange wallets. This makes trading more convenient and cost-saving. Transferring funds from exchanges to an independent crypto wallet and back again necessitates paying fees. Exchange wallets hold the users' assets as long they want and withdraw when they want to. They keep your trading funds safe and within reach.

Exchanges with secure wallets

Coinbase

Coinbase has a separate wallet service that is available in iOS, Android, and web browsers. The wallet was originally named Toshi before it became Coinbase Wallet. It was initially developed for Ethereum use and to have an interface that helps users to access DApps (decentralized applications).

Currently, the Coinbase wallet is one of the most trusted wallets in the crypto world. With millions of users across over 100 countries, this software wallet offers a higher level of security.

It has two types- the Standard Wallet which stores small numbers of cryptocurrencies and the Coinbase Vault which is ideal for storing a large number of coins and tokens. In addition, the Coinbase Vault offers two options- Group Vault and Individual Vault.

The advantages of using a Coinbase Wallet includes:

- It is a regulated wallet.
- It supports a wide range of crypto coins and tokens.
- It allows easy tracking of holdings via its proprietary platform.
- It offers an option to auto-send or receive funds.
- It is easy to use.
- Setup is free and simple.
- Recovery options are available
- iOS and Android compatible

Kraken

Kraken takes pride in having an integrated, strong, and very secure exchange wallet. It has a stellar reputation in the crypto industry and is one of the most trusted in Japan and European countries.

The majority of assets (95%) deposited by users are kept in cold storage or offline wallets to ensure their safety. The cold wallet devices are geographically distributed with 24/7 guards and security cameras. It only maintains enough funds in hot wallets within the system to sustain high liquidity and operations.

Here are the benefits you get when using Kraken Wallet:

- built-in crypto exchange functionality that allows users to trade anytime, anywhere

- allows fiat money withdrawal

- full SegWit wallet support

- extremely reliable and secure

- utilizes two-factor authentication

- employs API key permissions and account timeouts

- encrypts users' personal information

- reasonable withdrawal fee

Binance

Trust Wallet is Binance's official mobile wallet. It holds your crypto assets outside the trading platform and comes with built-in features that deliver a seamless experience.

This wallet offers the following benefits:

- It is multi-asset and all-in-one storage of your holdings.
- It supports over 40 blockchains and hundreds of thousands of coins and tokens.
- It is completely free with no hidden charges.
- Sending and receiving your cryptocurrency is fast and easy using QR codes, blockchain addresses, or address names.
- It is designed to safeguard your funds.
- It does not require personal data during the transactions, keeping your real identity hidden.
- Its decentralized nature allows you to have total control over your crypto funds and private keys.
- It comes with multiple card payment processors, letting you purchase altcoins and bitcoin without the need to leave the app.

- It supports crypto staking without any hassle.
- It has a built-in DApp (decentralized applications) browser on Android, allowing you to explore earning opportunities.
- It allows crypto swaps or exchanges.

Cex

CEX is a mobile exchange wallet that allows users to trade instantly and stores crypto for them. With the integration of a crypto exchange system, it allows you to trade your altcoins straight from the wallet, with no need to access a desktop or a laptop. It is ideal for day traders and active traders.

The benefits it gives include:

- client-level security measures (anonymity, strong data encryption)
- uses mobile and email verifications checking during the registration and initial logging in
- very strict Know Your Client requirements and regulations
- officially regulated
- stores most of the holdings in secure cold wallet devices

Bitfinex

Bitfinex offers 3 types of wallets to suit your needs – Exchange, Funding, and Margin.

- An Exchange Wallet is for buying and selling coins and tokens that the platform supports.
- A Funding Wallet is for providing funds or financing other margin traders. It is ideal for people who want to earn without active trading. This wallet allows you to offer your chosen terms such as amount to lend, duration, and desired return rate.
- A Margin Wallet is for margin trading, a type of trading that allows users to borrow funds from Bitfinex's P2P lending platform to leverage their positions.

Transferring funds from one wallet to another is free and simple.

Blockchain.com

Blockchain.com exchange offers lightning-fast trading of altcoins and supports 4 major currencies- USD, GBD, EUR, and TRY. Its proprietary wallet- Blockchain is one of the widely-used and trusted exchange wallets in the world.

It offers the following benefits:

- quick swap, buy and sell of coins and tokens
- allows the transfer of coins to the Interest Account to earn interests up to 13.5% every year, deposited monthly
- allows users to hold their private keys along with a Secret Private Key Recovery Phrase
- best-in-class crypto security
- supports clients in more than 200 countries
- is available in 25 languages

SPECIAL MENTIONS

Air-gapped crypto storage: Ellipal Titan

It holds the record of being the first air-gapped cold storage in the world, tamperproof, and with a full metal seal. It is waterproof, dust-resistant, and impact-resistant.

For data transmission, it does not need WiFi, Bluetooth, or USB. Instead, it uses generated QR codes, making it extremely safe and secure.

The QR codes format is transparent, controlled, and verifiable. For sending and receiving crypto assets, you need to connect this wallet with the Ellipal app.

Ellipal Titan has a built-in camera that scans QR codes and a huge touchscreen display. It stores the private keys offline, away from the prying eyes of hackers.

Any attempt to break it open triggers the deletion of stored private keys and causes the chip to erase every single data on the system. It costs $169.

Interest-earning wallet: BlockFi

Opting to store your altcoins in BlockFi Wallet allows you to earn interest up to 8.6% annual percentage yield (APY) through their BlockFi Interest Account or BIA. The interest is paid every month and accrues daily.

There is no minimum deposit required and the wallet is open to everyone who wants to own cryptocurrency. The app supports iOS and Android devices, letting you access your funds anytime.

All-in-one wallet: eToro

eToro is a multi-functional crypto wallet with great features that store your coins and tokens safely. It is also considered one of the safest hot wallets because of its high-level security components that prevent unauthorized access.

This includes strong DDoS protection, standardization protocols, and multi-signature facilities. It also allows existing users to access the cryptocurrency market.

It supports more than 120 cryptocurrencies and quickly converts over 500 pairs within the system. It offers a security key service when you accidentally lose or forget your private key.

Wallet with a Visa card: Wirex

It is perfect for people who are always traveling and want to trade wherever they are. Wirex offers safekeeping of your altcoins as well as letting you spend your crypto wherever a Visa card is accepted.

It converts your crypto at point-of-sale and gives Cryptoback rewards when you use this wallet when you pay online or in-store purchases. For maximum security of your altcoins, enable two-factor authentication.

DeFi wallet: Crypto.com

It is a non-custodial wallet that allows users to access DeFi services. The streamlined app lets you swap and farm DeFi tokens using this wallet.

A DeFi wallet has features to help you increase your yields by up to 20x. Crypto.com wallet stores your private keys and crypto. It gives you full control over your assets and holdings.

This wallet provides a 12/18/24-word recovery phrase, helping you import your current wallet. When it comes to security, this innovative wallet encrypts the private keys locally on your phone or computer with Secure Enclave.

It also uses 2-Factor Authentication and Biometric Authentication.

User-friendly wallet: Jaxx

Jaxx wallet has a user-friendly interface with clear text, pleasant colors, and an easy way to view the history of all your transactions.

It is best for both beginners and experienced users who like convenient features like QR scanning, access to the private keys and seed phrase, internal crypto exchange, multi-currency facilities, and cross-platform pairing.

Jaxx wallet is free for download and offers three options to complete transactions with varying fees that go direct to the blockchain miners.

Custodial Storage for Institutions and HNWI

Some exchanges specialize in giving custody services to High Net Worth Individuals (HNWI) and institutions.

The top exchanges that cater to the big players in the industry are:

- ✓ Coinbase – Coinbase Custody places crypto assets by storing them in segregated cold wallets. To ensure transparency, regular audits are conducted. Fund transfers are also being catered and customer support is always available.

- ✓ Gemini – It has two kinds of custody for virtual assets. One is the Deposit Custody, the default account that stores the users' funds in cold storage. The other kind is the Segregated Custody Account for the hedge funds of the institutions.

✓ itBit – It has an institutional custody service that allows clients to obtain and verify reports of their assets whenever they want. The assets are kept in cold storage and segregated. It also provides 24/7 support.

✓ BitGo – BitGo Cryptocurrency Wallet is the first multiSig hot wallet that is designed for institutional investors. The wallet's platform integrates your crypto into your investment portfolio, letting you transfer funds safely and easily.

It has advanced security configurations and multi-user policy control. BitGo has a BitGo Custody, BitGo Business Wallet, and BitGo Pay as You Go options to match your needs.

FAQs

Which is the best wallet for your altcoins?

There is no such thing as the best wallet. It all depends on your purpose for owning cryptocurrencies. For beginners who are looking forward to buying different kinds of coins and tokens, the best choices are Coinbase and Gemini wallets.

Is it necessary to have a crypto wallet?

It is not compulsory to have a separate crypto wallet if you are already using exchange wallets. However, getting a separate wallet to store most of your assets will keep them away from potential risks.

How to obtain a crypto wallet?

There are various ways to have a crypto wallet, including using the built-in wallets of the exchanges.

What is the best advantage of a software wallet over a hardware wallet?

Software wallets work like banking apps, allowing you to access your account via your smartphone or desktop.

Are software wallets safer than exchange/web wallets?

Software wallets or apps/programs that are installed in your mobile phone or computer are safer than web wallets. This is because the hacker needs to access your device to access the software.

Use 2-factor authentication and a strong password to protect you against cyber thefts and attacks. Moreover, do not lose your phone.

Is a hardware wallet worth the investment?

I highly recommend a hardware wallet, especially if you are into trading who want to transfer your profits to more secure storage. It is also best for investors of altcoins who prefer long-term or HODL investing.

How safe are hardware wallets?

Compared to software wallets, they are more secure. Hacking them remotely is quite impossible. They are also invulnerable to computer viruses that harm the software wallets.

Do I need more than one hardware wallet?

It is better to have 2 hardware wallets. The other one should be your backup if the one you usually carry or use is lost or stolen.

Why are hardware wallets called cold storage?

The physical aspects of hardware wallets enable usage even without internet connectivity. It makes them cold storage.

What is a multi-currency wallet?

A multi-currency wallet is a type of wallet that can store more than one type of coin or token. Some multi-currency wallets allow users to convert one crypto into another via the integration of the ShapeShift feature.

What is a MultiSig wallet?

It means a multi-signature wallet. This kind of wallet requires input or authorization from two or more parties to complete blockchain transactions.

Chapter 9

Should You Invest in Altcoins?

If trading cryptocurrency is not your option, you can still explore the potential of virtual assets by investing in alternative coins or altcoins. They are the stable coins, security tokens, and utility tokens, other than Bitcoin.

Like other types of investment, altcoin investment is long-term focused and ideal for people who want to grow their investment portfolio over time. The traditional way of investing uses stocks, bonds, commodities like gold and silver, and other asset classes.

In a gist, investing in altcoins depend on the following factors:

- Your financial goals
- Your risk tolerance
- Your knowledge about the cryptocurrency market and altcoins
- The time you can give in researching and monitoring your assets
- Your starting capital

At a glance

- ✓ **Is altcoin worth a try?**
- ✓ **What are the risks of altcoin investing?**
- ✓ **Guide questions**
- ✓ **Why are more investors choosing altcoins?**
- ✓ **Pros and Cons**
- ✓ **Is your crypto dead?**
- ✓ **Dead Coins**
- ✓ **Crypto investing mistakes to avoid**
- ✓ **Altcoin investing tips to help you dive in**
- ✓ **Frequently Asked Questions (FAQs)**

Is altcoin worth a try?

As an investment, altcoins have their own allure that attracts smart people. The most obvious is the higher percentage gain that crypto offers. This is why you should be investing in an altcoin that you believe is a good investment instrument.

Unlike trading that you are speculating or gambling, investing for a long haul is a smart decision which you should buy and hold.

o You should invest in a coin or token that you truly believe in and understand its true potential.

o It is crucial to research the people behind the altcoin, its value proposition, its performance history, trading volume, solidity, and more. With due diligence and a comprehensive study of different types of altcoins, you will find the coin/coins that match your criteria.

o Be wary of altcoins with low capitalization because they are prone to hacking attacks and market manipulation.

o Calculating how the risk factors will impact your invested fund is a strategic move you need to do.

o A worthwhile altcoin should offer the advantages you are looking for to ensure that your money is safe and will gain profit. You can begin by checking the top 10 coins in terms of market cap.

There is a continuing investor-driven demand for altcoins that significantly drive their value on the market. According to some market analysts, this investment trend works both ways- pushing the price up or plunging it down. It is up to the investors to speculate the direction of the altcoins. This short frenzy is also another indication to invest in altcoins, rather than trade and lose. Many altcoin traders are into long-term investment too, to diversify their strategies and holdings.

As more and more investors understand the true financial potential of altcoins and their real-life applications, the demand for altcoin investment is now growing steadily. In addition, the lower market shares of altcoin and lower prices compared to Bitcoin makes the yielding potential more profitable.

What are the risks of altcoin investing?

The main stimulus of investing in altcoins is the premise of 'room to grow' and is generally cheaper than Bitcoin. In the context of being cheaper, investors should remember that it correlates with lower market capitalization compared to Bitcoin.

In general, cryptocurrency is a volatile investment instrument. This encompasses all types of altcoins and tokens, including their big brother Bitcoin. There are many players in the market now and new types of altcoins are produced every day. Since there is no solid regulation about the creation of coins and tokens, the altcoin space is growing with alternative coins.

Altcoins are now occupying more than 40% of the total market cap of cryptocurrency. This makes it nearly impossible to directly say which among the many options is the best altcoin.

Another risk you have to consider is the lack of a regulatory body that governs altcoins. By being 'unregulated', there is a high possibility that you may lose your coins all at once and leave with nothing. You don't know where your money goes when you buy altcoins.

What you have in your digital wallet are numbers that represent the value of your investment and the guarantee that your invested fund is earning profits.

These risks should not be ignored and must be taken into consideration. Studying the security components and other risk-mitigating measures of the crypto exchange is very important to ensure that your holdings will be safe.

Guide questions that can help you decide to invest in altcoins

- Who are the people issuing and sponsoring it? What is their financial and technical background? How do they make money out of the transactions?

- What are your rights as an investor?

- When can you sell your investment? How can you sell it? What is the cost of selling it?

- Where is the invested fund going? How will they use it?

- What are the legal protections or safety nets that they offer in the event of malware, hack, or fraud attack?

- Who will refund your money when something happens? In case your rights are violated, are there adequate funds to commensurate you?

- Are they being audited on a regular basis? Who audits them?

- Do they issue financial statements?

Why are more investors choosing altcoins?

Altcoins quashed the Bitcoin monopoly of the crypto market, becoming optional coins for people who want to explore other investment tools. The altcoins rapid growth is due to their unique features which include having full blockchain technology, authenticity, and practical use in the market.

Altcoins cost less compared to Bitcoin, making them the perfect instruments for those who are still discovering the beauty of investment. Without paying the astronomical price, the promise of reaping huge rewards makes altcoins very attractive to financial-savvy individuals.

Other reasons are:

- **Altcoins grow fast**

  The rapid growth of altcoins gives pioneering investors a significant ROI.

- **Institutions and large companies start buying altcoins**

Ethereum, considered the second-largest crypto asset, is becoming the favorite of institutions and firms. In April, digital asset management company Coinshares reported that major institutions bought over $30 million worth of Ethereum. This brings the total holdings of institutional investors to $13.9 billion. Grayscale Investment Trust has also invested $1.5 billion in various altcoins including ETH.

- **The price surges of altcoins are higher**

Altcoin prices can surge more than the 20% market, depending on the uptrend factors. Moreover, DeFi trends are beginning to influence the altcoin market directly because investors can see their higher economic growth rate.

- **Altcoins are supported by reliable and popular exchanges**

Platforms with high liquidity and offers a wide range of altcoins like Binance, Coinbase, and Kraken prove the trustworthiness of the coins and tokens. Also, altcoins can be traded as Bitcoin pairs and purchased using fiat currencies.

- **Altcoins are legitimate coins for trading, hence good for investment**

  With the testimonies of people who profit in trading altcoins, the hesitancy to invest in them is becoming low.

- **Retail merchants and commercial businesses are now accepting altcoin payments**

  Aside from Bitcoin, the two altcoins that businesses accept as a form of payment are Litecoin and Ethereum.

> ### Did you know that?
>
> *Ethereum was proposed by Vitalik Buterin, a crypto programmer*
> *In 2013. During that time, he was only 19 years old.*

Risks and Opportunities

The altcoins' market is not yet mature at this point in time and everyone is still speculating on the future of cryptocurrencies. But the growing interest of people in altcoins and the proliferation of crypto exchanges/brokers is a manifestation that those with sufficient market liquidity will stay.

For those who are willing to take risks and discover the potentials of altcoins, understanding the risks and opportunities that it gives is important.

Opportunities

- Altcoins are regarded as the 'enhanced versions' of Bitcoin because they are created to provide the bitcoin's shortcomings

- Altcoins offer a wide selection of coins and tokens that delivers different functions

- Stablecoins, which are one type of altcoins, have the potential to fulfill the goal of Bitcoin as an acceptable medium for everyday transactions

- Several altcoins like XRP and Ether are trusted by mainstream institutions, gaining great traction and high valuations

- Higher risks can equate to higher rewards (with a big 'IF")

- Allows investors to get in early on projects that can immensely grow and gives 100x ROIs in just a matter of months

Risks

- Compared to Bitcoin, altcoins' investment market is smaller

- The smaller market capitalization and lower trading volumes make altcoins more susceptible to pump and dumps

- The variety of altcoins in the market makes it difficult to make a decision which is the best one

- Altcoins are impacted by the price of Bitcoin and momentum

- The lack of defined investment criteria and metrics as well as the absence of regulation give altcoins thinner liquidity and a lesser number of investors

- Altcoins are easily manipulated by bag holders and whale (big) investors

- A long term investment is incredibly risky because some altcoins lose their value as time passes by

- The reality of 'dead' altcoins that sunk the investors' money

Is your crypto dead?

Knowing that dead coins exist in the realm of crypto space helps investors make calculated and informed decisions. The tempting illusion of profitable crypto projects is constant and it is up to you to conduct extensive background checks on the projects. It is important to check their availability on major and trusted exchanges, their profit statements, and their trading volumes.

To spot dead coins, observe the active activities of the projects on social media platforms. Websites like Deadcoins and Coinospy track down floating dead crypto projects.

Some of the known dead coins are:

- **Aeron (ARNX)** was once a tradable coin on the Binance exchange but delisted after some time, causing the prices to drop up to 90%.

- **BitConnect (BCC)** enjoyed success during its first years but started to lose its credibility when UK financial regulators questioned its legitimacy at the end of

2017. In 2018, BitConnect was labeled a Ponzi scheme by Texas regulators, causing its eventual shutdown and the crash in the BBC price by 9%.

- **Storeum (STO)** died because of its lack of store value, zero liquidity, and dwindling market. The price of STO was $0.000012, but only 18 entries were recorded in its order book.

- **VegasCoin (VEGCOIN)** was a typical example of abandoned projects.

- **OxBitcoin (OxBTC)** was initially performing well in the market. The price soared to $5 but suffered a loss as the value fell to $0.10. The core team of the project left when it happened.

What are dead coins?

Crypto coins that are called 'dead coins' are those that suffered disinterest and eventual death due to a lot of reasons. The common reasons for their death include abandonment of key people in the project, insufficient funding or low liquidity, turning out to be scams, limited to zero listings on popular crypto exchanges, low trading volume, joke projects, and more.

In the crypto world, about 3.6% of the list of dead coins do not attract funding to support their development or offer lucrative profit margins.

Around 3% accounts to joke projects, while 6 out of 10 crypto coins with inferior liquidity and negligible trading volume are usually abandoned by the developers. Coins are considered abandoned or dead if their trading volume within 3 months is below $1,000.

The 2017 ICO craze rocked the crypto world when the number of coins gained momentum from 29 to more than 850 projects. Sadly, about 80% of the initial coin offerings were scams and left a trail of dead coins.

Nevertheless, new developers are all set to create new altcoins. In 2018, over 1,200 projects were launched. After two years, the total number of coins and tokens in the market is around 8,000.

With the proliferation of the wide variety of coins in 2020, another scam called 'rug pulls' resulted in another batch of dead coins.

Cryptocurrency investing mistakes that beginners should avoid

The continuous inflow of corporations and institutional investors raises the awareness of investing in cryptocurrencies, especially altcoins. The fact remains that the prices of these coins and tokens are dependent on public perceptions and speculations.

However, gauging how the fundamental factors influence the future performance of coins remains the most popular approach. By not following the basic guidelines, the possibility of portfolio losses is great no matter what kind of investment method you are using.

I rounded up the 5 worst investing mistakes you need to avoid as a crypto investor:

1. Buying crypto on speculation

Beginners are prone to this mistake, leading them to buy high and join the crowd that aims to gain big profits without considering the potential prospects of the coin or the factors that drive their price higher. Always remember that the cryptocurrency market is volatile and no one can predict the movements of their prices.

2. Low prices do not mean that the coins are cheap

Do not buy coins based on the promise of the creators that they will be the next 'bitcoin' and make you a millionaire in the near future. While it happens, like in the case of Dogecoin that experienced unexpected growth and made the investors instant millionaires and billionaires. But not every 'meme' inspired cryptocurrency has utility value or acceptability factor. In short, a low price typically reflects the actual worth and demand of the coin or token and not a discount.

3. Be guided by your risk tolerance

Always remember that you should not invest more than you can afford to lose. Investing is a speculative approach, where you win and lose. There is no sure guarantee of winning all the time. To mitigate losses, allocate funds that equate to your level of risk tolerance. Never, ever pull out other investments for the sake of leveling up your crypto portfolio. The smart move is to stick to long-term investments and put up a small percentage of crypto assets.

4. Always have an exit strategy before you buy altcoins

Purchasing an asset without exit plan is very risky. It is crucial for investors to have a solid framework or investment plan in advance that will stop high losses and achieve their financial goals. You don't invest your money to lose but to earn, so during the period when the market climate is becoming tougher, your exit strategies help you cut losses.

Exit strategies are also the keys to win more. Having a deeper understanding of market psychology and market sentiment makes smart investors decide to sell during the uptrends instead of holding their coins with the expectation of better price growth. If you want to squash losses and take advantage of gains, you should know when to sell.

5. Putting your golden eggs in a single basket

It is one of the worst mistakes that beginners can make. The hype of entering the world of crypto can be exhilarating and can make you invest big on a single popular coin only. But this approach can ruin your future investing and wealth plans. The better option is to spread your investment across or diversify your assets portfolio. In this way, you can mitigate major losses.

Newbies have a tendency to consider every price dip as a buying opportunity. They also believe that it is a good strategy to buy during the bull run or before the prices of altcoins become higher. Following these misconceptions would entail a higher risk of losing your venture capital. The key is always understanding why a bear or bull run is happening before investing big.

Altcoin investing tips to help you dive in

In May 2021, the total crypto value was over $2.5 trillion as more and more individuals, institutions, and companies joined the wagon. In another study, over 14% of adult Americans now own cryptocurrencies.

And while there are people who invest money to speculate, many are considering long-term investing because they see altcoins as a hedge against inflation and assets with store values.

Here are two ways to do it right:

1. Prepare for volatility and risks

Each coin or token has unique features that influence its price direction. This is why you need to have in-depth knowledge about a certain altcoin before you invest your money.

- Know the rationale behind the coin or token's creation

- Know the creators and major supporters of the coin including its governance structure

Understanding more about alternative coins can help you better diversify your portfolio and add crypto to your other holdings. It is important to embrace volatility issues and prepare for the best or worst. Preparation is always the key to reduce or prevent losses.

2. Learn the dynamics of the risk-reward concept

If you are all set to dive into crypto investing, remember that moderation is the key to success.

Limiting the percentage of crypto in your overall portfolio would not impact its risk-reward dynamics when the worst happened. One approach is through dollar-cost leveraging or investing a fixed amount regularly.

Quote

"Behind every crypto coin or token is a community."

FAQs

Are altcoins good investments?

Like Bitcoin, altcoin offers investment opportunities to those who dare but also risks that should be considered before taking the plunge. One key to preventing huge risk is trading well-established alternative coins with high liquidity and trading volume

Are stable coins really stable investments?

Stable coins are pegged to fiat currency or other investment commodities, making them a very good investment.

What are the coins that can help me diversify my investment portfolio?

Getting hold of any of the coins on the top 20 in terms of market cap, liquidity, and customer support. Bitcoin, Litecoin, and Etherum are always in the top 5.

Chapter 10

Other Key Concepts and Financial Lexicon in Crypto That You Should Know

Crypto Staking

Staking is a strategy that involves 'locking up cryptocurrency through Proof-of-Stake (PoS) consensus algorithm to earn passive income. The 'stake' serves as a validator to ensure the continuity, security, and integrity of the PoS network. In return, the validators or stakers receive newly minted coins.

How does it work?

- The participant supports the network by setting aside or locking up a certain amount of crypto coins/tokens.
- The staked coins will generate an active validating node on the blockchain.
- The higher the volume of coins, the greater the staking compensation or interest.

Many blockchains are now adopting PoS protocols as a response to the increased demand for cryptocurrencies. This innovative approach yields a higher annual percentage yield (APY).

You can stake crypto in 3 ways – via crypto exchanges, crypto wallets, and staking providers/pools.

1. Staking via crypto exchanges

- Binance offers flexible stalking or the staked funds are not locked and can be withdrawn by stakers anytime they want

- FTX locks staked coins within a certain period (fixed staking, but offers an option to instantly unlock them for a fee

- Bitfinex offers soft staking (flexible staking)

2. Staking from crypto wallets

The easiest way to stake your crypto is via altcoin wallets. The yields are much higher compared to staking in pools and exchanges. As long as you use a secure wallet, the staking risks are very minimal.

One example is Ethereum. You can stake your BNB (Binance Coin) using Trust Wallet and enjoy more than 23% APY based on the current computations. Using the same staking wallet, you can also stake TRX (Tron), CTX (Tesos), ATOM (Cosmos), KAVA, and ALGO (Algorand) to earn 6% to 12% APY.

Other popular choices are Ledger Wallet, Trezor Wallet, and Exodus Wallet.

3. Staking with dedicated staking providers or staking pools

- Staking providers offer a more comprehensive platform that allows crypto holders to lease nodes hosting and choosing coins they want to stake. It is best for large stakers. The most popular are Capital, Staked, MyCointainer, Stake, and stakefish. The most popular example is AllNodes.

- Staking pools work by allowing multiple stakers or validators to deposit their funds to increase the block rewards. By combining the computations resources to verify and validate new blocks in the network, the stakeholders get a share from the rewards. This option offers frequent staking income and more predictability.

What are the risks?

- Market risk – It refers to the potential adverse movement of the price of the staked coins/tokens.

- Liquidity risk – It is important to make sure that your crypto has a high trading volume and liquidity.

- Validator risk – It involves technicalities that can disrupt the staking process or the validator nodes.

- Validator cost – The costs you pay for running validator nodes (electricity/hardware) or percentage of the rewards can reduce your staking returns

- Lockup period – This staking option does not allow access to your assets for a specific duration of time.

- Rewards duration – Opting for long reward duration prevent stakers to reinvest the rewards, so choose assets that can give you daily staking rewards

- Theft or loss - Using a custodial staking platform that does not guarantee strong security is a red flag, so make sure that you go for staking wallets/exchanges/providers that are trusted and well-established.

> The hottest coins that offer big staking rewards are Ethereum 2.0, XTZ (Texos), ALGO (Algorand), ICX (ICON), ADA, DOT, ATOM (Cosmos), and NEO.

Decentralized Finance (DeFi)

DeFi is a peer-to-peer, digital financial services technology that allows crypto trading, interest accounts, and loan transactions.

It offers the following core benefits:

- True decentralization that dispenses third party interventions, censorship resistance, and global participation

- A non-custodial system that allows users to store their private keys and be in total control of their assets

- With blockchain as technological infrastructure, there is contract automation and immutability as well as low-cost, quick transactions

- Improved transparency protocols in the ecosystem that results in market and price efficiency.

- Favors network effects that generate innovations and combinations of projects in layer 2 and 3 applications

This blockchain-based concept of finance uses smart contracts rather than traditional financial instruments. Smart contracts refer to the set of special codes that automate the agreements between borrowers and lenders or buyers and sellers of digital currencies.

DeFi makes the assets open to the public decentralized network, allowing anyone to use the blockchain system instead of using middlemen. It utilizes technology to eliminate intermediaries and allow peer-to-peer transactions. All DeFi transactions and activities are done without the help of banks, exchanges, brokerages, and other financial institutions.

Other use cases that utilize DeFi:

- Lending and borrowing crypto to earn interest (via Aave, Dharma, Compound)
- Betting on the outcome of the events (via Augur, Synthetix, TokenSet)
- Buying Stablecoins that are pegged to a currency or commodity (via EOSDT, MakerDAO)
- Creating and exchanging asset derivatives like precious metals or fiat currencies (via Synthetix)
- Decentralized exchange of crypto (via Oasis, IDEX, Kyber)
- Insurance (via Etherisc)
- Taking part in a lottery (via Synthetix)

Quick facts

- The DeFi components are Stablecoins, a software track, and use cases

- The infrastructure and use cases of the DeFi ecosystem are still under development

- Oversight and regulation of decentralized finance are still lacking
- In the future, many believed that DeFi would replace the current rails of modern finance systems

- The primary exchange or network that supports decentralized finance activities is the Ethereum

- DeFi revolves around dApps or decentralized applications.

- Grayscale and other major asset management firms are starting to invest in DeFi technology

- As of March 2021, the total locked-in value of DeFi smart contracts was over $41 billion

-

Decentralized Applications (DApps)

In cryptocurrency, DApps or Decentralized Applications are digital protocols that run on a peer-to-peer (P2P) computing system or blockchain network.

They are often called smart contracts that distributed ledger technologies (DLT) like the Ethereum blockchain have popularized.

All DApps are executed and stored in the blockchain system.

Examples of DApps;

- Uniswap – decentralized crypto exchange
- Freelance – smart contract platform
- Augur – prediction market platform
- Blockstack – a platform that is designed for decentralized apps development
- Steem – a platform that rewards publishers with crypto token or coin
- Cryptokitties – Ethereum-based game

DDoS Attack

DDoS or Distributed Denial of Service attack happens when nefarious parties take advantage of the network by sending multiple requests. The goal is to overwhelm the website's capacity limit to handle transactions and from functioning properly.

DDoS is primarily accomplished using a network of remotely-controlled bots or zombie computers. Typically, the attack is focused on certain layers such as Layer 3 (the network layer), Layer 4 (the transport layer), and Layer 7 (the application layer).

Attackers target popular crypto exchanges in attempts to steal crypto or ask for crypto ransom.

Cybercriminals also use DDoS as a diversionary tactic while stealing data or installing malicious software to the website.

Quick facts

➢ In 2017, Bitcoin's system was allegedly attacked. It caused performance slowdown and left consequences in terms of processing volume and data storage. Since all blockchain transactions are irreversible and permanent, the false transaction during DDoS attacks would be stored on the system.

> ➤ Hongkong-based Bitfinex is a victim of several DDoS attacks (*source*: Twitter feeds showing seven attempts in 2016, seven attempts in 2017, and one attempt in 2018)

Initial Coin Offering (ICO)

ICO or Initial Coin Offering is one approach to raising funds for a blockchain project. It works by offering digital tokens.

Most ICOs are for ventures that are experimental, at an early phase of development, or have not started yet.

ICOs are high-risk, speculative investments that are not for faint-hearted people. There is a record of projects that take a number of years before becoming commercially viable. Some failed.

Risks to consider:

- Value fluctuation
  The value of ICOs greatly depends on their popularity, perceived value, ease of use, and underlying blockchain technology.

- Fewer safeguards

  ICOs are not regulated and highly speculative which can turn out to be scams, especially if it represents an overseas entity. ICOs are available online, sold globally, and paid with cryptocurrency, so when the issuers disappear after the fundraising, they are actually scams. Investors have little or no chance to get back their invested money.

GLOSSARY

A

Algo-Trading

Algorithmic trading is a trading system that uses automation to process the crypto orders of buyers and sellers. It uses algorithms or computer program rules.

Algorithm

It is a set of rules or processes that the computer follows to calculate operations or solve problems.

Arbitrage

Arbitrage is the strategy of taking advantage of the difference in the selling price between two exchanges. You buy a crypto coin or token from one exchange and sell it to another exchange for a profit.

Airdrop

Airdrop is a method of distributing tokens. It works by sending the crypto to a wallet address. It is often utilized for marketing functions like app downloads, referrals, and reshares.

Apeing

It is an approach that a crypto trader uses to buy a token from a project launch without in-depth research about it.

Ashdraked

It is the term used to describe the complete loss of the invested capital through a shorting approach.

ASIC

Application Specific Integrated Circuit or ASIC is a silicon chip that is designed for a specific task. In the context of crypto mining, the ASIC performs a calculation by finding values that deliver the necessary solution once it is placed into the hashing algorithm.

Atomic Swap

It refers to the crypto transfer from one user to another without the intervention of an intermediary or an exchange.

AMM

AMM or automated market maker refers to the system that gives liquidity to the crypto exchange.

B

Bag

It is cryptocurrency slang that describes a huge quantity of a certain coin or token.

Bagholder

A bagholder is a crypto owner or investor who buys and holds a large amount of a certain token or token.

Baking

It is a process that Tezos use to append new transaction blocks to its blockchain.

Basket

A basket is a collection of virtual currencies that are managed and considered as a single asset.

Bear Trap

It is a coordinated attempt of a group of traders to manipulate the price of a specific cryptocurrency.

Bearwhale

Any person that holds a large number of crypto and uses them to get a massive profit or drive their prices down.

Block

Block is a file with transaction data that is completed at a given time and becomes a part of the blockchain network.

Block Explorer

It is also called the blockchain browser or an application that allows users to check the details of the blockchain blocks.

Block Reward

Block rewards come in the form of coin and transaction fees that are given to miners after the transaction block has been successfully hashed. The reward composition depends on the cryptocurrency policy.

Blockchain Trilemma

It refers to the 3 issues that typically affect blockchains. They are security, scalability, and decentralization.

Bug Bounty

It is a reward given to someone who completed tasks research, design work, identifying code vulnerabilities, and more.

Bubble

It is a situation where the crypto is traded at a price that exceeds its intrinsic value.

Burned

Burned coins or tokens are those that are intentionally and permanently removed from the list of circulating crypto.

Buy Wall

It refers to the extremely big limit order that a trader places on an exchange.

C

Candlestick Chart

It is a graphing method that displays the changes in the crypto prices over time. A candle chart has 4 points of information:

- Opening price
- Closing price
- High
- Low

Capitulation

It refers to the process of selling crypto at a lower price, causing a significant loss. Traders capitulate when they believe or lose hope that the price of a certain currency will increase.

Central Bank Digital Currency (CBDC)

CBDC or Central Bank Digital Currency uses token or stablecoin to represent the digital form of a country's fiat currency. The idea is to create a legal tender that is regulated by a central bank.

CEX

Centralized exchange (CEX) is a type of crypto exchange that is owned and operated in a centralized manner.

Chain Split

It describes the separation of the original coin or fork into multiple independent projects.

Change

It is a concept used in cryptocurrency that utilizes the UTXO model. Change involves sending back coins to the crypto holder after using the unspent output to create a transaction.

Consensus

Consensus is the process that peers or nodes agree together and allow the transaction to take place. It is very important in the maintenance of the distributed ledger systems.

Coin

It is a cryptocurrency that operates independently. It also describes a single unit of the crypto.

Coin Mixer

It allows users to combine transactions to various addresses, making them untraceable and impossible to trace back the original sender or receiver of the cryptocurrency.

Coinbase

It is the number of coins generated from scratch in mineable cryptocurrency as a reward to miners for mining new blocks.

Confirmation

Every 10 minutes, a new block is mined. The block confirms the new transactions. Large transactions may require several verifications from a number of blocks. Once the transaction is confirmed, it cannot be double-spent or reversed.

Contract account

It is an account with associated code and crypto balance.

Core Wallet

It is a type of wallet that can hold an entire blockchain.

Crowdfunding

It enables companies, especially startups, to collect funds from supporters of the crypto.

Crypto Debit Card

A card that allows holders to pay for commodities and services using their crypto coins or tokens.

Cryptojacking

It involves using the computer of another user to mine crypto without permission.

Cypherpunk

A movement promoting crypto use and privacy-focused technologies in advancing political and social reforms.

D

DeFi Aggregator

It brings trades from different DeFi platforms in a single place.

Dead Cat Bounce

It is the term used to describe a temporary recovery after the prolonged price decrease.

Decentralized Social Media

It is a blockchain-based social media platform.

Deterministic Wallet

It is a crypto wallet where addresses and keys are generated from a single seed.

Difficulty

The difficulty is a concept that outlines the hardness of block verification during the mining process. In Bitcoin, the difficulty of Proof of Work mining changes every 2016 block. This is to adjust and keep the standard 10-minute block verification time.

Distributed Ledger

It refers to the system of recording the distributed information in different devices. The crypto blockchain is a distributed ledger that tracks all transactions.

Dumping

It is a collective sell-off of large quantities of crypto that are sold in a short period of time.

Dusting Attack

The goal of this attack is to discover the true identity of the owner of a crypto wallet, which in turn can be utilized in a phishing scam.

E

Encryption

It is the process that combines plaintext or document with the 'key' or a shorter string of data to create a ciphertext (output). Anyone who got the key can decrypt the output back.

Emission

The speed of the production and release of new crypto coins.

F

FOMO

FOMO stands for 'fear of missing out' where traders buy or sell crypto to gain profit during a bull period.

FUD

It is the acronym for 'Fear, Uncertainty, and Doubt.' This strategy aims to influence the traders' perception of a crypto market or a specific coin by spreading false, misleading, or negative information.

Fiat On-Ramp

It is one way to get crypto coins from fiat currency.

Fiat-Pegged Crypto

It is an asset, coin, or token on a blockchain that is connected to a bank-issued currency.

Fish

It refers to the person with a small cryptocurrency investment.

Futures

They are standardized legal agreements to sell or buy a certain asset at a specified time and price in the future.

G

Genesis Block

It is the initial data block that is computed in the blockchain network.

Gems

The term 'gem' is used to describe unknown low-cap crypto coins that are undervalued but have great potential

Governance Token

It is a token that represents a voting right to influence the crypto ecosystem.

H

Hash

Hash refers to the function that accepts input and generates an alphanumeric string output called 'digital fingerprint' or 'hash value'. Each block in the crypto network has a hash value that validates the transaction.

Hashing

Hashing refers to the mining process that uses cryptographic hash functions to solve mathematical problems.

`

Halving

Halving is an event that impacts the supply and demands of mined cryptocurrencies like Bitcoin and Ethereum. It is basically the process of halving the mining incentives after a certain number of blocks is achieved.

Hybrid Consensus Model

The Hybrid Consensus Model uses both Proof of Work (PoW) and Proof of Stake (PoS) consensus. This mechanism brings balanced network governance by allowing blocks to be validated by miners and voters (stakeholders.)

Honeyminer

It is a crypto mining app that users can download on multiple devices.

In-the-Money/Out-of-the-Money

They are two trading mechanisms that give options to investors to use and harness the benefits of additional tools.

I

Infinite Mint Attack

It occurs when a hacker or an unwanted person mints a great number of tokens within the network's protocols.

Initial Dex Offering (IDX)

An IDX or initial dex offering is an option used by companies instead of an initial coin offering (ICO).

Initial Exchange Offering

It is a form of crowdfunding that start-ups in crypto generate funds by listing in the exchange.

Initial Token Offering (ITO)

An ITO is like an ICO but offers tokens that hold intrinsic utility value (either through usage or software in the ecosystem).

Instamine

It is a term used to describe the distribution of a large portion of crypto right after its public launch.

Intrinsic Value

In cryptocurrency, the asset's intrinsic value refers to its actual worth that is determined by a financial calculation instead of its present price.

J

JOMO

It stands for 'Joy of Missing Out,' which is the opposite of FOMO (fear of missing out).

K

Kimchi Premium

It is a phenomenon that makes the valuation in South Korean exchanges appear higher compared to other global crypto exchanges.

L

Ledger

It is the record of financial transactions that can only be appended when there are new transactions in the blockchain network. It cannot be changed or edited.

Light Node

It is a downloaded wallet that is connected to full nodes. It further validates the stored information on the blockchain.

Liquidity

It is the term used to signify how easily a coin or token can be sold or purchased without influencing the overall prices in the market.

M

Malware

Malware is malicious software or harmful computer program that can compromise the operations of a server, network, or computer.

Margin Call

The value of the investor account is less than the margin maintenance amount.

Market cap

Market capitalization or market cap is the total capitalization of the coin or token's price. It is used to rank the crypto's relative size.

Mempool

It is a collection of unconfirmed transactions in the node.

Merkle Tree

It is a cryptography tree structure where each leaf node is labeled with the data block hash while the non-leaf node has the hash of the label's child nodes. It helps in the secure and efficient verification of the blockchain content by propagating the change upward toward the top hash.

Mining Difficulty

It refers to the difficulty of finding the next block's right hash.

Mining Farm

When a group of crypto miners work together for a purpose or achieve a goal like energy use.

Mining Reward

It is a reward that miners get for mining a new block.

Mining rig

It refers to the equipment that miners use for mining crypto.

Moon

It is a situation that displays an ongoing upward movement of the crypto price.

N

Network

It is the nodes in the blockchain that work to process and validate transactions.

Nodes

Nodes are computers that connect the crypto network. The nodes work to relay and validate transactions while keeping the blockchain copy. There are two types of nodes:

- Full node – A computer that can fully download blockchain's complete data and fully validate crypto transactions.

- Lightweight node – This type of computer uses a different process of validation and cannot download the entire data of the network.

O

Open Source

It is a concept where participants believe in an open and free sharing of information for the greater common good.

Option

It is a contract that gives the traders the right (not an obligation) to buy or sell the underlying instrument or asset at a strike price.

Oracle

In the blockchain network, the oracle refers to the machine or human that relays the data to the smart contract, which in turn verifies the outcome of an event.

P

P2P

Peer-to-peer or decentralized interactions of two parties in the blockchain.

Permissioned Ledger

A permissioned ledger is owned by one person or group of people. Any access to the network or ledger is given by the owners. Permissioned ledgers run faster and are easier to maintain compared to public blockchains. The data of this type of ledger is highly verifiable and accessible to all parties.

Ponzi Scheme

It is a fraudulent investment strategy that promises returns to investors from funds that new investors contribute.

Private Blockchain

It is a distributed ledger (blockchain) with a closed network and is controlled by one entity. New participants require a verification process and have the capability to limit the number of people who can participate in the validation process.

Private Currency

It is a token or currency that is issued by a private company or person. Usually, a private token or currency is used within the private network only.

Proof of Authority

It is a consensus mechanism that grants a private key to a private blockchain. It allows the blocks to validate the cryptocurrency transactions.

Pump and Dump

Pump and dump refer to the investment scheme that a participant or participants group does to artificially raise the asset's value so they can sell their coins at a higher price.

R

Recovery Seed

A cryptographic security code that is composed of 12 to 14 random characters.

REKT

It is the slang for 'wrecked', which means that the investor has lost substantial money.

Rug Pull

A type of scam where crypto developers take the investors' money and abandon the project.

S

Seed Phrase

It refers to the single starting point in getting the keys of a deterministic crypto wallet.

Serialization

It is the process that converts the structure of data into byte sequences. Ethereum, for instance, uses RLP (recursive-length prefix encoding) encoding format.

Sharding

It refers to the splitting of the network into 'shards' or portions. Every shard comes with a unique set of smart contracts and account balances.

Shitcoin

A coin with no usage or potential value.

Slippage

The situation where traders have to pay a different amount for their purchased crypto because of the sudden price movement.

Smart Contracts

Smart contracts are self-executing coded agreements between crypto buyers and sellers. Once the predetermined conditions on the contract are met, the contracts automatically complete the process without intermediaries.

In a gist, smart contracts are relatively straightforward and trustless.

Smart Token

It is a token with value and has the key information necessary to simultaneously execute transactions.

Soft Cap

It refers to the minimum amount that ICO aims to raise.

T

Transaction Block

It refers to the set of network transactions that can be hashed or added to the blockchain.

Ticker Symbol

It is a unique letter combination assigned to crypto or stock, making them identifiable on trading apps and exchanges.

Token Generation Event

It refers to the time when a token is publicly issued.

TVL

It is the total value locked (TVL) that represents the number of assets being staked in a certain protocol.

Trade Volume

It is the amount of crypto that is being traded in the past 24 hours.

Trading Bot

It is a program that automates the crypto trading of assets on a trader's behalf.

U, V, W, X, Y, Z

Unspent Transaction Output (UTXO)

It refers to unspent transactions that are left after all the transactions are completed.

Vanity Address

A crypto public address where letters and numbers are chosen by the owner.

Vaporware

A crypto project that never happens.

Volatility

It is the statistical measurement of returns dispersion that uses the standard variance between returns and the market/security index.

Wash Trade

It is a type of market manipulation where investors make artificial activity by buying and selling similar crypto simultaneously.

Whitelist

It is the list of registered participants who are interested in ICO.

Whitepaper

A document that provided technical information and a growth roadmap of the crypto project.

Zero Confirmation Transaction

It means unconfirmed transactions on the exchange.

Conclusion

Thank you for reading my book.

After reading all the chapters of **Cryptocurrency Trading Guide to Altcoins & Bitcoin for Beginners**: *Learn about Decentralized Investing Blueprint, Cryptography, Blockchain, Mining, Ethereum, Litecoin to Create Wealth. Best Trading Strategies,* I hope you are more equipped and prepared to begin your journey to success.

My personal journey to crypto trading begins by learning the basics. I am a learner of life, of exciting rides to create more wealth. And I believe that every one of us has this thirst to gain more, be more, and earn more. Trading and investing are two ways to achieve it fast. But it is not for weak-hearted people. It works for people who are not afraid of the myriad of trading risks and are willing to experience loss when they hit the worst.

And for the more courageous, cryptocurrency is the new player in the game. It promises a great return on investments and grows your wealth in no time at all. But it has its own set of risks that can wipe off your capital or investment. Your ticket to success is to learn all the facets of crypto trading and decentralized investing.

As more and more individuals and companies are exploring the real-world application of decentralized investing and trading in blockchain technology, expect more amazing things to happen. You can be a mere observer or ride the tide and become a player.

Again, my gratitude for making this book part of your wealth journey. I wish you success and good riddance!

Made in the USA
Coppell, TX
17 October 2021

64222081R00193